The Vagus Nerve Anxiety Relief Playbook

Take Back Control in Just 7 Days—The Proven Protocol to Eliminate Anxiety Without Drugs, Therapy, or Feeling Helpless Again

Marina Heathcroft

TABLE OF CONTENTS

INTRODUCTION

Your alarm buzzes and you're already bracing for the rush ahead—family breakfasts, looming deadlines, the swirl of city traffic. You pour your coffee and feel, almost imperceptibly at first, your heart speeding up, a faint jitter in your stomach. By the time you step into that crucial meeting or face a tense conversation with a loved one, your mind is spinning through worries and what-ifs. Maybe your breath grows shallow, palms slick with sweat, shoulders tensed as if holding up the sky. It's moments like these—unseen by all but deeply felt—that shape the undertow of modern life. If you've ever wondered why reassurance alone rarely brings relief, or why anxious thoughts are so hard to out-think, you are not alone. This scenario isn't just common; it's part of how our bodies have been wired to keep us safe—even when comfort, connection, and calm are what we crave most.

What few realize in the midst of this everyday storm is that the body makes the first move. Long before your conscious mind crafts a story about fear or failure, your autonomic nervous system has signaled a shift—heart racing, stomach fluttering, breath catching. At the center of these changes sits a remarkable nerve: the vagus. Known as the 'wandering nerve' for its winding path from brainstem to gut and beyond, the vagus acts as a hidden conductor orchestrating your mood, digestion, energy, and sense of safety. Scientists have discovered that strengthening this pathway—through specific breathwork, gentle movement, sound, even cool water on the skin—can dramatically reduce anxiety's grip and speed recovery from daily stressors. In fact, adults with higher vagal tone bounce back from intense stress 40% faster and enjoy more resilient moods. This isn't hopeful thinking; it's measurable biology. When you learn how to work with your nervous system, you open the door to real, sustainable change.

This book was created for those seeking clarity and confidence, not just another list of self-help tips. Inside, you'll unpack the science behind anxiety and the vagus nerve, discover practical daily habits honed by research, and learn step-by-step protocols to steady your body and mind. Whether you want less anxiety, deeper sleep, steadier moods, or more ease in supporting your family, what follows is an invitation to reclaim agency over your well-being.

These pages offer straightforward routines for busy lives, plus strategies to personalize each tool so progress sticks—no matter your age, ability, or health history. By the end, you'll not only understand how your body shapes your feelings, but hold an actionable roadmap to make calm a lived reality.

If you're skeptical, overwhelmed by conflicting guidance, or wary of pie-in-the-sky wellness promises, your caution is welcome here. Many readers arrive burnt out by advice that doesn't fit their bodies or feels unreachable amid full schedules and complex histories. Others worry that new techniques could backfire or aren't sure how to adapt them safely for themselves or their families. This book meets those concerns head-on: every chapter includes trauma-aware language, inclusive options for varied backgrounds and sensitivities, and clear guidelines for adapting practices to your unique needs. You'll find stop-rules, consent checks, and easy-to-follow signals for knowing when to pause, swap, or seek extra care—all grounded in medical evidence, not wishful thinking.

I'm Dr. Morgan L. Hayes, an integrative physician blending two decades of neuroscience, mind-body medicine, and trauma-informed care. My clinical practice bridges medical science with holistic therapeutics, and I've worked alongside somatic therapists, dietitians, and biofeedback specialists to support adults navigating stress, anxiety, and chronic illness. This book draws directly from evidence-based protocols, clinical experience, and collaborations across specialties—so every strategy you try comes with both rigor and compassion. I understand the realities of juggling career, caretaking, hormonal shifts, and the relentless pace of urban (and family) life. My promise: you'll never be asked to ignore discomfort or push past healthy limits. Every step honors your dignity, autonomy, and need for safety.

The journey ahead is practical and empowering. First, you'll get a new lens on anxiety—why it's more than a mental loop and how early physical cues shape our experience. From there, we'll dive into the core science of the vagus nerve and heart rate variability, breaking down big concepts into plain English. The central toolkit chapters walk you through breathing, cold exposure, touch, sound, and mindful movement—offering scripts, illustrations, and digital downloads for easy learning. We'll then explore tailored protocols for high-stress spikes, user-friendly device options, and real-life resilience-building routines. Finally, you'll find guidance for personalizing and stacking practices, integrating lifestyle basics like nutrition and sleep, and tracking progress without overwhelm. Each section builds on the last, taking you from foundational skills to advanced tools in approachable steps.

What sets this resource apart? Safety and inclusion aren't afterthoughts—they're built into every protocol. Expect clear guardrails for those with trauma, chronic illness, or sensory sensitivities, along with adaptations for pregnancy, menopause, and different body types. Holistic wellness isn't an add-on: gut health, sleep rhythms, light exposure, meal timing, and even hydration intersect with nervous system care throughout. Every technique is presented with evidence citations and troubleshooting for common stumbling blocks. Visual guides and an online companion library mean you can access help whenever you need it, at your own pace.

Here, nuance and science sit side by side—a book made as much for skeptical thinkers as for curious explorers.

You picked up this book because you want more control, more peace, and new possibilities for yourself and those you love. Change starts now. As you turn the page, give yourself credit for showing up and being willing to learn something different. You don't have to memorize neuroscience or become a meditation expert. Instead, you're about to gain simple, powerful practices—tools you can use anywhere, anytime, to restore calm and build lasting resilience. This journey is yours: respectful, flexible, and designed for real (sometimes messy) lives. Take a slow breath, loosen your jaw, and let's begin together. Relief and confidence are possible—not in some distant future, but starting today.

Chapter 1

RETHINKING ANXIETY: YOUR NERVOUS SYSTEM'S MISSING LINK

You've probably heard the phrase "Anxiety is just overthinking," and perhaps you've tried to calm a racing heart or ease a tight chest by talking yourself through it. Maybe before an important meeting, that sudden drop in your stomach or pounding in your chest made you search for a reassuring thought, only to find the feelings growing stronger instead. What if these physical sensations are not the result of anxious thoughts, but rather the sparks that ignite them? Long before your conscious mind notices a worry or panic, your autonomic nervous system has already triggered changes in your body—heart rate spikes, breathing quickens, muscles tense—all happening in mere milliseconds. This means anxiety starts in your body first, and your thoughts follow after, trying to make sense of what your nerves have already set in motion.Understanding anxiety as a bodily experience that precedes mental patterns opens up a new path to relief—one that is quicker, simpler, and more dependable. When you shift your focus from chasing down anxious thoughts to noticing and gently adjusting your body's signals, you step into a different dialogue with anxiety. This chapter invites you to explore anxiety through the lens of biology, revealing how your nervous system orchestrates these early warning signs and why recognizing this hidden connection can transform the way you manage stress. By seeing anxiety as your body's message rather than just your mind's story, you gain tools to interrupt the cycle before it spirals, making calmness not a distant goal, but an accessible, natural state.

Anxiety Reframed Through Biology

Imagine you're waiting in line at the grocery store. Your heart suddenly starts pounding, palms go clammy, and your breath moves high into your chest before you've even had a chance to register any single worrisome thought. This is your body's stress response kicking in, often far ahead of your awareness. These automatic states fall under what's commonly called the fight–flight–freeze response. When your nervous system senses a challenge—real or imagined—it prepares you to deal with it by triggering sympathetic arousal. In this state, your heart rate goes up, breathing becomes quick and shallow, and your vision narrows as if you're peering through a tunnel. You might find yourself restless, fidgety, or filled with a sense of urgency.

Sometimes, though, if escape or fighting feels impossible, another pathway takes over: dorsal vagal shutdown. Here, your limbs can feel heavy, movements slow, thoughts drag, and there's a pull to disappear, withdraw, or lie down. This freeze response, also known as hypoarousal, may show up as numbness, emotional flatness, or even a sense that you don't quite exist inside your own skin *(Dorsal Vagal Shutdown:*

How to Recognize When Your Nervous System Shuts Down, 2024; The 3 States of Anxiety in the Nervous System - Therapy in a Nutshell, 2022). These patterns happen in fractions of a second—well before stories about danger or failure flash across your mind. It isn't that anxious thoughts cause these bodily shifts. Rather, those physical shifts create a stage for anxious thinking to take over.Your nervous system works like a two-way highway between your body and brain. Around eighty percent of nerve traffic on this highway heads from your organs back up toward your brain, not the other way around. Most of what influences your mood, alertness, and sense of safety starts in your body. This flips the old idea of "mind over matter" on its head.

Sensations like a fluttering stomach, a tight chest, or a rapid heartbeat serve as signals that call your brain to attention.

The brain interprets these signals and scans for reasons behind them, often filling in the details later. When you learn to soften how your body experiences anxiety—for example, by taking slower, deeper breaths—your brain starts to receive "it's safe now" messages. Gradually, the spiral of worry eases its grip. All of these messages rely on a pathway where one particular nerve carries most of this body-to-brain information—a topic you'll explore more in the next section *(Dorsal Vagal Shutdown: How to Recognize When Your Nervous System Shuts Down, 2024)*. Taking action at the body level leads to clearer thinking and helps regulate the cycles of anxiety that can feel so relentless.It's not just feelings and tension that travel this highway—it's your thoughts as well. The state your body sits in shapes the story your brain tells. High sympathetic arousal primes you to see neutral or even positive events as threats. An email from your boss suddenly seems loaded with criticism, or a late train makes your mind rush to worst-case scenarios.

Everyday stressors feel bigger when your body's in full alert mode. On the flip side, when your system drops into dorsal shutdown, your thinking tends toward hopelessness and withdrawal. Minor setbacks trigger thoughts like "Why bother?" or "I can't handle this," even if you managed tougher days before. These responses don't come from personal weakness or character flaws, but from automatic survival mechanisms *(Dorsal Vagal Shutdown: How to Recognize When Your Nervous System Shuts Down, 2024; The 3 States of Anxiety in the Nervous System - Therapy in a Nutshell, 2022)*. When you first work with your body's state, mental reframes become possible because your nervous system is no longer working against you. Relief comes not from arguing with your thoughts, but from shifting your state together with them. There's real hope built into your biology. Thanks to neuroplasticity, your nervous system can change and adapt throughout life. Every time you practice calming your breath, gently return your attention to the present, or use grounding touch, you lay down new pathways in your body and brain. These routines strengthen your capacity for calm in the same way regular exercise builds muscle. Even a couple of minutes a day can lead to changes within weeks. Old wiring driven by past stress doesn't have to call the shots forever—patterns can shift with repetition and kindness toward yourself *(Dorsal Vagal Shutdown: How to Recognize When Your Nervous System Shuts Down, 2024)*. The daily practices detailed in Chapters 3 through 6 build directly on this principle of trainability, sending steady signals of safety that help your nervous system get better at finding calm. Your baseline isn't fixed or doomed by genetics. With small actions repeated over time, your inner world grows more flexible and resilient.

Meet the Vagus Nerve

Think of anxiety as a physical state that sweeps through your body, not just a mental storm. This happens because your body's internal wiring—the autonomic nervous system—sets off stress alarms and resets calm signals. At the heart of this network runs the vagus nerve, a long, paired bundle that stretches from the brainstem down into the chest and deep into the abdomen. Like a superhighway, it sends signals that slow the heartbeat, deepen breaths, move food along in the gut, and dampen inflammation (Keer, 2024; Capilupi et al., 2020). When the vagus nerve is communicating smoothly, you feel steady, your heart rate finds a gentler rhythm, your breathing feels open, your digestion settles, and the background sense of tension fades. These shifts don't stay hidden; they spill over into how calmly you face challenges, how easily you let go of worry, and how clearly you think when under pressure.

Ventral vs. Dorsal

The vagus nerve isn't just one switch—it has two main branches with very different effects. When the front branch, or ventral vagal pathway, leads the way, you're set up for connection and safety. Your gaze softens, your voice carries warmth, your breathing falls into an easy flow, and your body feels anchored. You notice small joys, you want to reach out and be social. On the flip side, when the dorsal branch takes charge, everything slows and shuts down. Eyes lose their sparkle, words dry up, energy drops away, and limbs can feel heavy or numb. In this state, it's hard to muster motivation or interest, and even small tasks might seem overwhelming. Learning to spot which branch is running the show gives you the power to choose better coping strategies. If you catch yourself in a shutdown, gentle movement or simple sensory cues can help lift the fog. If anxiety feels hot and swirly, calming practices like breath work can nudge you back toward balance. Knowing these bodily cues guides the practical work ahead.

Heart–Brain Rhythm

Every moment, the vagus nerve shapes subtle shifts in your heartbeat and breathing. Scientists often talk about "vagal tone," meaning how much sway the vagus nerve holds over your heart and organs. A person with high vagal tone bounces back from stress more quickly because their body relaxes and recovers more quickly (Keer, 2024; Capilupi et al., 2020). Heart rate variability, or HRV, is another way to see this in action. Instead of your heart ticking like a metronome, a healthy body lets the time between beats wiggle in response to emotions and activity. Think of HRV as built-in flexibility—a sign you can shift gears without getting stuck. Higher HRV goes hand in hand with easier recovery from upset, clearer thinking, and even better sleep. Breath practices have been shown to boost vagal tone and increase HRV within minutes, laying the groundwork for fast-acting strategies you'll try later in this book.

Modulating Stress Fast

Signals travel along the vagus nerve in moments, not hours. Take a slow exhale, hum a note, or splash cold water on your cheeks—these actions can send instant quieting instructions straight through your nervous system, dialing down alarm states in real time (Keer, 2024; Capilupi et al., 2020). As heart rhythms steady and muscles unclench, the brain gets the message: It's safe to stop scanning for danger.

Catastrophic thoughts fade, and the urge to escape or shut down melts away bit by bit. These rapid shifts aren't just interesting—they are your ticket to taking command of anxious patterns, building motivation, and making change stick.Feeling this fast feedback is what makes quick wins so motivating—and why your next step matters.

Why Quick Wins Matter

Given the vagus nerve's ability to rapidly alter autonomic output and shift your state in moments, it makes sense that brief interventions aren't just convenient—they are wired into your body's design. When stress rises, your nervous system signals change in a matter of seconds. These fast signals open up an opportunity: a window where you can disrupt anxiety before it locks you into loops of catastrophic thinking or avoidance behaviors. The practices you're about to discover build on this biology, showing you how to press pause on the spiral with something as simple as a slow breath or a subtle shift in posture (Bentley et al., 2023).

Before you try these rapid techniques, it's helpful to understand how quick wins set the stage for lasting change—and why the right guardrails make them safe and reliable.

Safety First, Always

Before you dive into the practices that create those quick wins, remember that relief is most reliable when it comes with a sense of control. The excitement to feel better is real, yet safety matters more than speed. Everybody reacts differently to new sensations, so finding your own safe zone is just as important as learning any technique. You are not expected to get everything perfect immediately; taking small steps keeps your system steady and helps you listen to what feels right each day.

Chapter 2

HOW CALM WORKS: THE SCIENCE OF VAGAL TONE AND HRV

Imagine wearing a device that quietly tracks your subtle body signals and reveals surprising insights into your stress levels and recovery. In a group of people using these wearables, those with the highest heart rate variability, or HRV, experienced nearly half as many days filled with intense anxiety compared to those with the lowest scores.

Not only that, but they also bounced back from stressful moments 30 to 40 per cent faster. Even a modest increase in HRV over two months was associated with better sleep quality and more peaceful mornings. These findings highlight vagal tone — the strength of a key nerve pathway that controls our body's calm response — as a real, measurable path to building resilience against daily stress.

Vagal tone is the body's built-in calm system, playing a central role in keeping us grounded through life's ups and downs. This chapter breaks down what vagal tone means in everyday terms and why it matters. By understanding how the system works, you'll see the science behind your numbers and discover simple practices to strengthen your vagal tone—turning abstract data into practical steps for daily calm and balance.

Vagal Tone Decoded

A strong vagal tone significantly reduces anxiety days, speeds up recovery from stress, and promotes steadier moods—these are not random effects. In the top quartile of HRV scores tracked in the chapter summary, people saw a 48% drop in high-anxiety days, faster stress recovery, and more stability throughout daily challenges. Vagal tone acts like the dial on your body's calm response. When set higher, it keeps the brakes ready to slow your heart, settle breathing, and restore clear thinking when startled. This isn't out of reach; wearables show that with steady practice, anyone can move this dial and see real changes in mood, energy, and resilience (Keer, 2024; Lopez Blanco & Tyler, 2025).

The most immediate way vagal tone shows up is in the 'rest–digest' response: it restores calm after a stressful event. Think about your body after a startling phone call or tough meeting—heart pounding, shoulders tight, shallow breath. If your parasympathetic brake is strong, it steps in quickly.

Your heart rate slows, breath deepens, a sense of relief washes over, and worries lose their grip. This recovery is natural and automatic for those with higher vagal tone, just as responsive brakes let a car stop smoothly at a light. For others, the brakes feel worn: stress lingers, recovery takes longer, and each ripple leaves a bigger mark. Simple actions done every day—like three slow belly breaths after closing an email or splashing cold water on the face—train this system so the next wave of stress passes quicker and leaves less tension behind (Keer, 2024; Lopez Blanco & Tyler, 2025).

Social engagement forms another bridge between vagal function and daily life. The ventral vagal pathway, which supports safe connection, lets facial muscles relax, brings warmth to your voice, and makes it easy to look someone in the eye during conversation. When this branch hums along, social moments flow: laughter comes easily, misunderstandings fade, and even uncomfortable silences feel bearable. But if this part of the system is quiet, people sense it right away—words get clipped, tone flattens, shoulders inch up, and making small talk feels almost impossible. Every day, anxiety often hangs here, making friendly faces seem distant or social cues hard to read. Small habits like slowing your exhale while speaking or using a soft gaze before meetings wake up these calming circuits, helping you feel at ease around others—social tools detailed further in Chapter 3 (Keer, 2024; Lopez Blanco & Tyler, 2025).

Vagal tone also taps into the body's inflammation brake. At the cellular level, the vagus nerve communicates directly with immune cells, dialling back the release of inflammatory chemicals called cytokines. The outcome is far more visible than it sounds: fewer tension headaches, less joint pain, and less stomach unease signal that background inflammation is down. Low-grade inflammation can feel like a constant hum—a sense of irritability, restlessness, and fatigue that mimics and magnifies anxiety. By training your vagal tone through gentle rituals like paced breathing, light movement, or even humming, you keep this anti-inflammatory line open, supporting a more comfortable, stable baseline. Here, the vagus nerve links emotional steadiness and physical health, weaving together mind and body as introduced in Chapter 1 (Keer, 2024; Lopez Blanco & Tyler, 2025).

For digestion, vagal tone sets the pace and rhythm. A responsive vagus helps meals move along, smooths stomach emptying, and keeps bloating at bay. Stomach flips, cramps, or a knotted gut are common when the tone runs low—often during periods of chronic stress. This is the gut-brain axis in action: when digestion is peaceful, calming signals travel up the vagus to reassure the brain, lowering feelings of threat and dampening anxiety. A simple pre-meal ritual—three slow breaths, dropping the shoulders, drawing out the exhale—primes vagal tone before eating. This settles nerves, promotes easier digestion, and creates a moment of comfort at mealtime (Keer, 2024).

All these effects—faster stress recovery and better digestion—point to a key, trainable quality: vagal tone. Understanding what this system controls helps you track progress. The most practical tool for this is heart rate variability (HRV), which wearables measure and will be discussed next (Lopez Blanco & Tyler, 2025).

Heart Rate Variability in Plain English

Imagine your nervous system as a car equipped with a smart shock absorber. Vagal tone acts like this suspension—absorbing stress, smoothing out the ride, and helping you recover after bumps in the road. Heart Rate Variability, or HRV, is the number on your dashboard that tells you how well these shock absorbers are working at any given time (Narjisse Damoun et al., 2024). For many people, seeing a graph or score for HRV can feel intimidating—like staring at a complicated engine diagram when all you want is to know if your car will get you home safely. In truth, HRV simply translates the invisible work of your vagus nerve into an easy-to-track sign of resilience. The higher your HRV, the more flexibly and rapidly your body can return to calm after a challenge.

Picture driving over a rough road. With good suspension, your car glides over potholes; with poor suspension, every bump jolts you. Your heart behaves the same way. While your average heart rate might be steady, the tiny differences—the micro-wiggles—between each beat show how adaptable your body is (Tiwari et al., 2021). This "healthy wiggle" in heart rate means your system constantly adjusts speed, pressure, and readiness. A flexible heart (high HRV) lets you shift smoothly from work focus to relaxation at home, or handle a surprise calmly. If your variability drops (low HRV), it's like losing the shock absorber: you get stuck in high alert, recovery feels slow, and even small stressors can rattle your system. Instead of imagining a perfect rhythm, think about a rhythm that subtly changes moment by moment. This adaptability signals your vagus nerve applying just the right amount of "brake" when you need it most (Narjisse Damoun et al., 2024).

HRV looks different for everyone, and that's normal. Young adults, athletes, and anyone who regularly moves their body—walking, dancing, cycling—tend to have higher baseline HRV than older adults or those just starting to build fitness (Tiwari et al., 2021). Hormones also play a role: menstrual cycle phases can slightly raise or lower HRV from week to week, so comparing numbers across phases may not give a clear picture. There are typical patterns—higher HRV in the follicular phase, for example—but your trend matters most. Sex-related differences exist, too, yet the range within any group is broad (Narjisse Damoun et al., 2024). Comparing your scores to professional athletes or much younger folks misses the point. Your HRV today versus your HRV next month is where growth shows up; make yourself your own reference point.

Some days, your HRV will dip regardless of effort—maybe due to poor sleep, fighting off illness, or emotional stress (Narjisse Damoun et al., 2024). One low reading isn't a crisis. Instead, notice how your HRV moves over a week or two. Are you staying about the same, drifting upward, or dropping? Tracking a 7-day or 14-day rolling average helps smooth out daily noise and points toward real improvement. Consistency counts far more than hitting a high score once. If you see steadier numbers or a gentle climb, you're building the kind of responsive nervous system that supports long-term resilience. Celebrate these shifts, however small—they signal that your practices are making an impact.

Every day choices influence HRV far more than most people realize. Deep, restful sleep consistently increases HRV by allowing the parasympathetic system to reset and repair (Tiwari et al., 2021). A single night of poor sleep can drop your numbers, while a stretch of solid rest brings them back up. Hydration matters too: drinking enough water and getting minerals like sodium and potassium help regulate blood pressure and support healthy heart rhythms, which protect HRV (Narjisse Damoun et al., 2024). Alcohol has a rapid effect—it tends to push HRV down for a night or two, even with moderate intake. The menstrual cycle is another normal source of fluctuation; tracking HRV alongside cycle symptoms can help you spot natural dips and practice self-kindness rather than blame. By attending to sleep, hydration, alcohol choices, and cycle awareness, you find levers that enhance both your HRV and your daily experience of calm and energy.

With HRV demystified, the next step is learning how your breath can immediately nudge these numbers in a calming direction.

Breath–Heart Synchrony

While tracking HRV trends reveals your nervous system's flexibility over days and weeks, your breath offers something even more immediate—a real-time lever you can pull to shift your state within minutes. Each inhale and exhale performs a subtle dance with your heart rate, creating a rhythm the body knows well. This is called respiratory sinus arrhythmia—the natural rise and fall of your heartbeat that matches your breathing cycle. When you inhale, your heart beats slightly faster; when you exhale, it slows down again. Place two fingers on your wrist pulse and breathe naturally—you might feel the beat grow a little quicker as air fills your lungs, then soften and stretch as you release. This rhythm isn't just a curiosity. It's the sign of a responsive, healthy nervous system (Gerritsen & Band, 2018). Noticing this wave in your own body is an easy way to tune into safety signals. Even just a few minutes focusing on this movement—during anxious moments or stressful transitions—can build confidence that you have influence over how you feel inside.

Heart rate variability, the measure discussed earlier, reflects the flexibility of this breath–heart partnership. Research has shown that slow, deliberate breathing practices boost parasympathetic tone—the calming branch of your nervous system (Gerritsen & Band, 2018). Regular breathing rhythms help your body switch out of urgency and settle into steadier functioning. As you move forward, the principles here form the foundation for the quick-reset breathing techniques you'll practice later.

Extending the exhale amplifies this effect. When you exhale, vagal signalling increases, sending a powerful message to your body that it's safe to relax. Try breathing in for four seconds and out for six or eight, letting your exhale go soft and unforced. You might want to include a gentle one- or two-second pause at the end of each breath, which isn't about holding or straining, but about noticing the peaceful space after the breath leaves. This pattern can ease nervous urgency without making you feel dizzy or deprived. Many people find it helpful before difficult conversations, while waiting for an important email, or as part of a bedtime wind-down. Studies support that even short sessions of breathwork—five minutes a day—shift mood and reduce physiological arousal, with longer exhales being especially effective at calming the system (Balban et al., 2023; Pramanik et al., 2009; Bernardi et al., 2001).

Breathing through your nose gives your body a physiological edge. The nose warms, filters, and humidifies air, easing the load on the rest of your system and supporting smoother oxygen exchange (Gerritsen & Band, 2018). Nasal breathing also encourages the diaphragm to drop and the belly to expand, helping to loosen chest tightness that often pairs with anxiety. If your nose feels stuffy, try brief nasal breaths—20 to 30 seconds—and experiment with posture by sitting tall or gently tilting your head until breathing eases.

This allows you to work up gradually as comfort grows. There is no need for all-or-nothing thinking—adapt as needed.

Gentle practice always wins over forceful effort. For sensitive bodies, rapid or forceful breathing patterns can sometimes mimic panic symptoms, such as lightheadedness, tingling fingers, or the urge to gasp. Instead, let your jaw soften, let your belly stay loose, and aim for breath that feels quiet, smooth, and sustainable. Comfort-first cues like these keep you grounded and help avoid alarm signals triggered by sharp shifts in carbon dioxide levels. Light, unhurried practices are no less effective—they're kinder and better suited for long-term self-regulation (Gerritsen & Band, 2018).

You may notice barriers on some days—blocked sinuses, heightened awareness due to trauma history, or discomfort focusing on breath. Honour this wisdom. Experiment with shorter intervals, take breaks, or place a comforting hand on your chest as you breathe. Every attempt at synchronizing breath and heart builds familiarity and trust in your body's ability to reset. Once you feel your pulse ease with each exhale, you'll want simple ways to notice whether these shifts are adding up—which is exactly what the next section's minimal tracking approach will show you. This growing sense of agency is the gateway to the skill-building toolkit ahead.

Measuring What Matters

Now that you understand how breath steers your vagal brake in real time, the next step is capturing whether these micro-adjustments translate into lasting change—without turning your day into a data obsession. Tracking nervous system health should feel supportive, not stressful. With so many apps, numbers, and devices available, it's tempting to monitor every heartbeat or mood swing. But for those living with anxiety, relentless self-checking can do more harm than good. Sustainable calm grows when tracking stays light, simple, and kind.

Three core signals form an approachable dashboard: sleep quality, morning mood, and resting heart rate. These markers catch the most important shifts without demanding constant attention. Sleep quality reflects how well your body recovers overnight—a direct window into parasympathetic activity and vagal tone. Just rate your sleep each morning as poor, okay, or good. No need to analyse cycles or graphs. Use a notebook, phone app, or even sticky notes by your bed.

Resting heart rate reveals long-term trends in autonomic stability. Count your pulse for sixty seconds before getting out of bed or checking your phone. Place two fingers on your wrist or the side of your neck, set a timer, and record the number. If you have a wearable device, its overnight average works too. Consistency matters more than the method. Morning mood and body sensations bring in context that only you can sense. Note one word like "tense," "loose," "heavy," or "light." This fast check-in helps connect physical states to daily patterns. Keeping the process quick and judgment-free encourages honesty while lowering perfectionist pressure *(Resting Heart Rate before Bed: The Ultimate Sleep Metric • #1 Continuous Glucose Monitoring App Australia | Vively, 2025; Shaffer & Ginsberg, 2017)*.

Tracking well doesn't mean tallying up every moment. Instead of minute-by-minute monitoring, use structured checkpoints once per week to see how things are really shifting. Pick one regular time, like Sunday night, and spend ten minutes looking over your week's entries. Write two or three sentences: what helped, what got in the way? For example, "Evening humming made me fall asleep faster; late-night scrolling kept my mind wired." Or "Morning walks made my mood lighter; skipping breakfast left me sluggish." This small ritual keeps your efforts focused and sustainable, stopping the shame spiral that comes from missing a few days. Clarity comes from step-back reviews, not from chasing after every little detail. Weekly summaries give your mind space to notice trends and celebrate signs of progress without triggering anxious loops.

Calm isn't just about what happens overnight—it's also about what changes in the moment. Before and after any breath, movement, or relaxation practice, rate your calm and tension on a scale from 0 to 10. Jot the numbers quickly before and after a three-minute session. Look for shifts of 1 to 3 points rather than expecting big leaps. Small, steady positive changes build trust in yourself and the practices you're using. Not every session will move the needle, and that's normal. Some days, a three-point drop happens; other times, just one point shows up. Both are real signals. When the numbers don't shift for several tries, tweak one part of your routine. Maybe try a longer out-breath, adjust your posture, or pick a quieter spot. See what moves your scores gently over time, treating the process as a science experiment rather than a test you can fail. Self-kindness makes this learning loop much more effective *(Resting Heart Rate before Bed: The Ultimate Sleep Metric • #1 Continuous Glucose Monitoring App Australia | Vively, 2025)*.

Simple tracking opens the door to meaningful personalization. Over time, let the signals guide subtle tweaks instead of giant overhauls. If you see low heart rate variability and poor sleep together multiple mornings, prioritize wind-down routines and lighter dinners. If social plans often lead to tense reactions, schedule five minutes of gentle breathing or a walk beforehand. Give yourself a full month between bigger changes, keeping what works and adjusting only one thing at a time. Your data becomes your personalised roadmap, showing where to lean in or pull back. These simple tracking signals will guide you in the next chapter as you select breath, touch, and movement practices tailored to your unique nervous system profile.

What matters most is staying curious and letting your own experience shape your approach. There's no perfect scorecard, only evidence of what steadies you over days and weeks. Missed logs or wobbly patterns aren't setbacks—they're just honest parts of the journey. By choosing three clear signals, reviewing progress weekly, and rating calm and tension simply, you give your nervous system space to restore itself—not just in numbers, but in lived experience (Shaffer & Ginsberg, 2017).

Chapter 3

BUILDING YOUR CALM-FIRST TOOLKIT

You've probably tried calming techniques like deep breathing, only to end up feeling dizzy. Maybe you've taken cold showers that made your heart race instead of calming you down, or tried long meditation sessions that tested your patience. When anxiety hits out of nowhere, like in a checkout line or right before a Zoom call, the last thing you need is a complicated routine or tools that make things worse. This isn't about a lack of willpower or effort. Often, the real problem is that the practice you picked doesn't fit your situation or how your nervous system is working at that time.

This chapter gives you simple, flexible tools to help with this problem. You'll learn how to choose practices that fit your life, schedule, surroundings, and how your body feels. When you know how to match calming methods to your situation, you can pick what works best, avoid frustration, and get better at finding calm that lasts.

Choosing Practices That Fit Your Life

When you try self-calming techniques, you might find that what you need doesn't match what feels safe or possible.

Many people feel dizzy, lightheaded, or anxious with cold face plunges or rapid breathing. These methods aren't bad, but they might not fit your nervous system, schedule, or location. The goal is to help you choose practices that fit into your day and work with your body, not against it.

Time Boxes: Start With What's Realistic

The first step is to align your practice with the time you have. You don't need a whole hour. What matters is finding something you can do most days. Being consistent builds resilience more than how long you practice (Debnath, 2022). Here are three levels to consider:

30-Second Shifts: Use these when you only have a moment, like waiting for water to boil or at a red light. Try a long exhale: breathe in for 3 seconds, then slowly breathe out for 6, noticing your belly relax. You can also tap each finger to your thumb, counting up to four and back. Even blinking slowly and paying attention to the feeling can help calm your nerves.

Two-Minute Pockets: These are good for times like waiting for a meeting or sitting in your car. Try gentle neck stretches, sipping warm water slowly, or a quick body scan by noticing where your body touches the chair, your feet on the floor, and your hands in your lap. Another option is slow sighing: breathe in through your nose for two seconds, then let out a soft sigh for six seconds. This helps calm your stress response (Lindsay et al., 2018).

Five-Minute Recalibrations: Use at home when you need a full reset, such as after a tough conversation or before bed. Lie down, place both hands over your stomach, track your breath, and count ten slow cycles. Pair this with soft background music or the scent of orange essential oil, which studies link to decreasing stress hormone spikes (Debnath, 2022). Planning these windows makes practice easier to maintain in daily life.

Context Match: What Works Where

Besides time, your surroundings and who's around you affect what feels safe. Social comfort is just as important as the calming tool. If you're worried about looking strange, your anxiety can get worse instead of better (Debnath, 2022).

Public Spaces: Try subtle techniques that don't stand out. You can rest your eyes softly by looking to the side, count silently, or touch your fingertips together in your pocket. Quietly noticing sensations, like "cool air" or "weight in feet," helps you stay grounded without anyone noticing.

Commute Settings: During a subway ride or in traffic, sound-based resources like gentle playlists via headphones, synchronized foot tapping, or slow nasal breathing offer relief. Gentle neck turns, barely tilting side to side, or squeezing a soft ball in your bag can be grounding while avoiding stares.

Home Base: At home, you can use more visible tools like lying down for progressive muscle relaxation, humming, splash-washing your face, or using aromatherapy. Home is also the best spot to try slightly stronger interventions, like holding a warm mug or applying a cool washcloth to your forehead. Just remember, practices should never increase distress or discomfort.

Trigger Awareness: Know Your Personal Red Flags

It's just as important to notice what triggers your anxiety. Not every vagus nerve technique feels safe for everyone. If your comfort zone is small, as explained in Chapter 1, some practices like ice water dips or long breath holds might make you feel more anxious instead of calmer (Lindsay et al., 2018).

If cold makes you feel jumpy, use lukewarm water instead and focus on making your exhale longer. If long breath holds make you panic, keep your breaths short and gentle, or try sensory grounding, like rubbing a smooth stone or noticing the air on your skin. These are just ways to adjust, not signs of failure. Your body knows what helps and when it's time to try something different.

Stacking With Habits: Make Practice Automatic

To make these practices automatic, add them to routines you already do. Research shows that new habits stick better when they're tied to something steady (Debnath, 2022). For example, do a breathing exercise while your coffee brews: close your eyes and count three slow breaths. On your commute, let every fifth streetlight remind you to drop your shoulders and relax your jaw. At bedtime, wiggle your toes as you turn off the lamp and notice how your legs feel.

Connecting a practice to a regular moment helps your body expect it, making it easier to keep up. In the next section, you'll see how changing how often and how intensely you practice can make each technique work even better.

After you've chosen practices that fit your time, situation, triggers, and routines, the next step is to figure out how often and how intensely to use them for the best results.

The Dose–Response Curve of Calm

Now that you've found techniques that fit your schedule and setting, it's time to figure out how much to do them for the most benefit without overwhelming yourself. Many people think doing more is better, but your nervous system improves with steady, manageable steps. Knowing how much, how often, and when to rest makes any practice safer and more effective.

Low and Slow Start

Starting with less than you think you can handle helps you build a strong base. It's like weight training: lifting too much too soon can cause problems and slow you down. With calming practices, pushing to your limit can make you feel anxious or irritable. The 50-70% rule helps: if you think you can do five minutes, start with two or three. Let your body get used to this first. Change only one thing at a time, like making it a bit longer, stronger, or more frequent. For example, if you're doing breathwork, keep the intensity and number of breaths the same while you slowly add time.

After each session, check in with yourself. If you feel calmer, stick with that level. If you still feel tense, do less next time. This gentle approach helps you stay steady both in the short and long run (Hamdani et al., 2022).

Frequency Beats Length

Doing short, frequent sessions helps your nervous system learn better than doing long practices once in a while. It's like learning a new skill: five one-minute tries each day work better than one long session a week. Your body's calm system responds best to repeated patterns. Try 30 to 90 second mini-practices throughout the day, like after reading emails, before meetings, or after lunch. You don't need extra time; just fit these into your daily transitions. Aim for 15 to 20 sessions a week, so you don't stress about missing a day. Over time, these small, regular doses help your body adapt and give lasting relief from stress and anxiety (Evans et al., 2021; Hamdani et al., 2022). A sixty-second humming or slow exhale, done several times, can make a bigger difference than a long routine that feels overwhelming.

Recovery Windows

Balancing activity and rest helps keep your nervous system from getting more stressed. Some calming techniques, like humming, cold exposure, or shaking, can make you feel more alert if you do them back-to-back without a break. After each active practice, take 30 to 60 seconds of quiet time. You can look softly at the wall, listen to gentle sounds, or take a few deep breaths. If you do several techniques in a row, add a one- or two-minute pause between them so your body can catch up. Try to keep all your practices in one sitting to ten or fifteen minutes at most, since too much can make you tired or irritable. These breaks aren't wasted time; they help your body learn to feel safe again (Evans et al., 2021).

Signs of Overdoing

If you notice jaw tension, headaches, feeling tired, or a sudden spike in anxiety, these are signs you need to go easier. Too much stimulation, even with calming techniques, can backfire if your system can't handle it. If you notice these signs, cut your session time in half or pick a gentler version, like humming softly instead of loudly or doing fewer repetitions. Always follow active work with rest.

Keeping a diary of your time, intensity, and techniques can help you see patterns and adjust your limits. The goal isn't to be perfect, but to notice what works, make changes as needed, and treat these adjustments as progress, not failures (Hamdani et al., 2022).These dosage principles give you the 'how much' and 'how often'—next, you'll define personal signals that tell you when to continue, modify, or stop entirely. With consistency and calibration, the path to greater calm becomes sustainable in even the busiest lives.

Creating a Safety Net Plan

Knowing how much to practice is only part of staying safe with anxiety. It's just as important to notice when your body needs a break or a change. Safety boundaries aren't there to hold you back—they help you trust yourself and your process, so each step feels steady and safe (Derricks et al., 2025). Signs like jaw tension, headaches, and tiredness are early warnings from your nervous system. When you pay attention to these signals and set clear rules for what to do, your toolkit becomes something you can count on.

Define Green–Yellow–Red: List Your Bodily Cues for Each Zone

Begin this exercise by finding a quiet moment and grabbing a notebook or your phone. Imagine three zones: Green, Yellow, and Red. Green means you feel calm, Yellow is a warning zone, and Red means you need to stop right away. List three physical cues that tell you your body feels safe: maybe steady, easy breathing; warm hands; clear focus; or relaxed shoulders. For Yellow, list warning signs such as shallow or quick breath, restlessness in the legs or fingers, tightness in your jaw, or distracted thinking. These mean your nervous system may be tipping out of its comfort zone, calling for less intensity, shorter duration, or a gentle pause. In the Red column, write clear stop cues like dizziness, chest pain, a sudden surge of panic, or feeling frozen. One strong signal per zone is enough to start with. Over time, you may notice more patterns, but this first map gives you practical decision points. Keep your chart somewhere handy, in your notes app or on a sticky note, so it's easy to check during practice.

Feeling safe isn't just a mental experience; it's rooted in your body's biology and shaped by neural circuits that read cues of safety and threat (Porges, 2022). When you use this Green–Yellow–Red system, you turn abstract concepts into real-world anchors. Even small shifts, like noticing your hands getting clammy or your breath tightening, can guide your choices and support well-being. This self-mapping also helps prevent overwhelm, since you'll always have permission to adjust or stop before distress escalates (Derricks et al., 2025; Porges, 2022).

Stop–Swap–Soothe: Choose a Gentle Backup (e.g., Hand-on-Heart) if Triggered.

Next, create a backup plan—a simple way to feel safe again if you hit a Red zone. Think of "Stop–Swap–Soothe" as your emergency plan you can use anywhere. First, stop: If you notice a Red sign, pause, press your feet to the floor, and name five things you see around you. This helps bring you back to the present. Next, Swap: Switch to a backup practice, like putting your hand on your heart and slowing your breath, or humming softly to yourself. Choose one gentle move now and write it down, so you're ready when you need it. Finally, Soothe: Add a comforting touch, like a palm on your cheek or hand behind your neck. Stay with this for 10 to 20 seconds, then rate your distress from 0 to 10.

This helps you decide if you're ready to continue, need more time, or should ask for help. Practice this sequence every few days when you're calm, so it becomes a habit for stressful times.

This approach is based on the idea that your body uses safety signals to regulate itself. You don't shift states just by willpower, but by simple actions that tell your nervous system you're safe (Porges, 2022). Having a plan ready helps stop fear from taking over and gives you a sense of control.

Support Script: Write a 2-Sentence Self-Talk Line You'll Use When Anxious

When anxiety hits, what you say to yourself matters. Make a two-sentence support script. Start with a short, non-judgmental line, like "My body is signaling stress; I can respond gently." Then add a simple action and next step: "I'll take four slow breaths and relax my jaw; then I'll re-check in one minute." Keep your script under 20 words so it's easy to remember. Save it on your phone, a wallet card, or your bathroom mirror. This isn't just positive thinking—it's a proven way to break worry and guide your nervous system with kindness (Derricks et al., 2025).

Personal self-talk scripts work best when they help you accept your body's signals and suggest a gentle next step. Research shows that feeling emotionally safe helps your body stay balanced and supports good self-regulation (Porges, 2022).

Check-In Alarm: Set Two Daily Reminders for a 30-Second Body Scan

Early intervention prevents escalation. Set two alarms at times that fit your routine—perhaps at 9 a.m. and 3 p.m.—and label them "Body Check: Jaw, Shoulders, Breath." When each alarm goes off, scan your body for tension, posture, and breath. In the morning, check your jaw and shoulders, then take three long exhales or roll your shoulders if tension rates 3 or above out of 10. In the afternoon, scan hands for warmth, stomach for softness, and breath depth.

Adjust your evening plans if you detect any Yellow signals. Stick with these check-ins for at least seven days, honoring the reminder even when it seems unnecessary. Regular self-monitoring teaches your nervous system to catch trouble early and return to a safe state quickly (Porges, 2022).

These daily habits slowly change how you relate to anxiety and your body. Mapping, scripting, practicing, and checking in build a flexible safety net, making each vagus nerve practice safer and more effective. Once you know your personal limits, you'll be ready to track your progress with more confidence, knowing each session stays within your safe zone for growth and recovery (Derricks et al., 2025; Porges, 2022).

Baseline Assessment Snapshot

Now that you have a safety net plan, it's time to figure out your starting point. Tracking your anxiety each day helps you see what's really happening in your body and mind—no judgment, just information for you. This isn't about diagnosing or labeling yourself. It's about getting a clearer picture to guide your choices and help you notice real progress as you go (Balaskas et al., 2024; Beltzer et al., 2023).

Pick three steady times each day to pause—morning, midday, and evening work well (like 9 a.m., 2 p.m., and 8 p.m.). If these don't fit, feel free to pick your own set routine. At each checkpoint, stop for ten seconds. Notice where any tension sits in your body, how your breath feels, your thoughts—don't try to change anything, just witness. Rate your current anxiety from 0 (completely calm) to 10 (maximum distress). Add one or two sensation words—"tight shoulders," "racing heart," "warm cheeks," or whatever fits best. Jot this down on your phone's notes or on paper, or use the printable tracker from your digital resources. Seven days of these snapshots give you enough information without turning tracking into a chore. The aim here is curiosity, not perfection—missed entries don't matter.

After the week, draw a simple line graph or mark out numbers visually so you can spot peaks and dips. Where does anxiety rise—mid-morning, post-lunch, late at night?

These patterns offer clues about rhythms in your nervous system. High numbers aren't failures; they're signals that you have busy internal weather. This map helps you choose when to insert calming techniques for stronger results (Beltzer et al., 2023).

Top Triggers: Zeroing In On Spikes

Look back at your seven-day ratings. Find moments when your number jumped two points or more within an hour—these are likely triggers. Bring the situation to mind and pinpoint the context. Examples might include: sitting in traffic on the morning commute, prepping dinner while kids call for homework help, waiting for feedback after a difficult meeting, or scrolling through social media before bed. Make a short table for each:

The situation/context (be concrete, like "standing in checkout line during grocery rush")

Time of day and who else was present (if relevant)

Body sensations (clenched jaw, buzzing fingers, butterflies in the stomach)

Be specific: "work stress" is too general, but "prepping slides with a deadline and team chat pinging" is something you can act on. For each main trigger, choose one small preventive practice, like a sixty-second 4:6 breathing cycle in your car before going inside, three slow sighs before opening an email, or a hand-on-heart pause before setting boundaries at home. The goal isn't to fix yourself or avoid all discomfort, but to be ready for the moments you know are tough (Balaskas et al., 2024).

Top Soothers: Charting What Calms You

Think about times when your anxiety went down on its own. Maybe you were humming to music, walking outside, stretching your neck, or drinking warm tea. Write down three things that usually help you feel better, even if it's just for a minute or two. Try new tools from this book, like gentle humming, cool water on your wrists, or a butterfly hug. After two minutes with each, rate how well it worked from 0 to 10. Notice if each one helps right away, lasts longer, or works best in certain places (some may be better for quiet rooms than busy commutes).

Keep your list of soothers somewhere easy to find. For each one, note the technique, whether it calms sudden anxiety or helps you feel steady for longer, and if you need any props or privacy. Some favourites, like rhythmic breathing, work well in public, while others are better for quiet time at home. Place reminders where you'll see them—a travel compress in your bag, sticky notes by your mirror or desk, or breath-pacing audio on your phone. Your toolkit works best when you know what fits your own rhythm (Beltzer et al., 2023).

First Experiment: A Gentle Test Run

Select one gentle, accessible tool from earlier sections—4:6 nasal breathing or hand-on-heart plus slow breaths are both solid choices, easy to integrate and low-risk. Link your experiment to a daily habit: after making coffee, during lunch, or as part of your bedtime ritual. Before you begin, rate your anxiety (0–10) and jot down one or two body cues. Practice for two minutes, then re-rate and note any change.

At the end of the week, figure out your average anxiety ratings before and after each practice, and the difference. If your anxiety drops by two points or more, this tool is a keeper. If there's little or no change, adjust your approach—try a different time of day, practice for three minutes, or switch to another gentle tool next week. Every result matters: even when something doesn't work, it helps you find what does (Balaskas et al., 2024).

Doing this assessment is a way to be kind to yourself. Tracking isn't about earning gold stars or pointing out mistakes. By noticing your patterns, choices, and real reactions, you become your own expert and supporter. Keep your baseline sheet handy—on your bedside table, in your phone, or in your book. Plan to check in again in two weeks, comparing your morning, midday, and evening ratings to your first set. As you approach your ups and downs with curiosity, you'll be ready for the next chapters and can choose the practices that fit you best.

Chapter 4

BREATH AS A SWITCH: FAST AUTONOMIC RESET

At precisely 2:10 p.m., Maya finds herself parked just outside her office, feeling the familiar surge of anticipation that tightens her chest and sends tingling sensations to her hands. Her smartwatch registers a heart rate of 98 beats per minute as she braces for an important call scheduled in five minutes. To steady herself, she sets a three-minute timer and begins a deliberate breathing pattern: softening her belly against the seat belt, drawing a quiet four-second inhale through her nose, followed by a calm seven-second exhale. After completing six cycles of this focused breathing, she introduces three physiological sighs—each composed of two brief nasal inhales paired with one long, slow mouth exhale. The tension begins to fade as her shoulders relax and a gentle warmth radiates through her chest, while her heart rate drops noticeably to 78 bpm. When the call begins, Maya feels composed—not because the stress disappeared, but because she skillfully engaged her body's autonomic reset.

This chapter unpacks the techniques that enabled Maya's rapid shift from anxiety to ease. You'll explore how extending the exhale acts as a direct switch for calming the nervous system, grounding it in clear physiology rather than wishful thinking. From learning the mechanics behind exhale-weighted breathing to practicing resonant breath cycles and the physiological sigh, these methods offer practical tools to downshift stress in moments when you need it most. By understanding how breath influences your body's natural wiring for safety, you'll build a reliable pathway to navigate tension and reclaim stability quickly and effectively.

Physiology of Exhale-Weighted Breathing

Building on what you learned about vagal tone and measuring your baseline, this section shows how breath can shift the body's stress response in real time. You've already seen how the window of tolerance opens and narrows depending on autonomic state; now, you'll discover why exhale-oriented breathing becomes a direct dial for nervous system reset—especially in moments when anxiety threatens to spill over.

A longer exhale naturally brings calm, acting like a brake on anxious momentum. With each out-breath that extends beyond the in-breath, the vagus nerve signals 'stand down' to your heart and digestive organs. This isn't just psychological—it's visible as respiratory sinus arrhythmia: your heart rate rises slightly on every inhale and slows on every exhale.

When practicing a 1:2 breathing ratio (such as inhaling for 4 seconds and exhaling for 8 seconds), the pause and lengthening of each exhale give your body more opportunities to shift towards recovery and away from fight or flight modes (Miranda, 2023; Ma et al., 2024). Imagine moving through stair laps or a brisk walk: matching movement with slow inhales and even slower exhales lowers both pulse and blood pressure, softens tense muscles, and often clears racing thoughts within two minutes. Your mind feels less cornered, and warmth spreads into your belly and shoulders. These changes aren't forced; rather, you're aligning with the body's natural wiring for safety and restoration.

Breath that is low, slow, and quiet sends a very different message to your brainstem than quick, shallow panting. Diaphragmatic breathing causes your lower belly to gently rise, drawing air deep where baroreceptors reside around the heart and major vessels. These pressure sensors report back to your nervous system: all is well here. Using your nose filters and humidifies incoming air and creates slight resistance, helping to pace each inhale without gulping. Air enters quietly, the chest barely lifts, and the belly expands sideways like an accordion. The neck and jaw stay loose, so there's no bracing or tightness—a gentle fullness replaces the urge to gasp. Each breath feels softer, as if coaxing relaxation rather than chasing it. When airflow is nearly soundless, it breaks the loop between anxious thinking and breathlessness. This way, the act of breathing itself reassures and grounds you (Miranda, 2023; Ma et al., 2024).

Sometimes, the urge to take bigger, faster breaths creeps in, especially under stress. Fast or deep breaths may seem soothing at first but can actually lower carbon dioxide levels in the blood—a state called hypocapnia—that triggers lightheadedness, tingling, air hunger, and chest pressure.

These sensations feel alarmingly similar to panic. Mouth breathing tends to make overbreathing worse, since air enters too easily and too much. If you notice yourself getting dizzy or feeling desperate for air, pause. Swallow once to reset your airway, then begin again with smaller, slower nasal breaths, letting the belly guide the movement. Notice any urge to override the process. Remember: spotting and adjusting these patterns is part of mastering the skill, not a setback.

Posture lays the groundwork for how breath feels and flows. A soft, ungripped belly lets the diaphragm move downward fully with each inhale—think of loosening a belt notch or allowing the waistband to relax. Keep your jaw unclenched, tongue resting softly against the roof of the mouth, and lips gently together. Visualize stacking your spine so your ears rest over your shoulders, and your shoulders float above your hips. As you breathe in, let the ribs widen to the sides rather than puffing up the chest. This open, supported alignment makes it easier to let go of effort and allows the breath cycle to unfold effortlessly. Instead of managing or controlling breath, posture invites it. A relaxed frame conserves energy, making extended, calming breaths sustainable across movement or stillness.

Once you grasp why the exhale calms and how gentle mechanics keep anxiety in check, you'll be ready to apply these principles in a structured resonant breathing session. Soon, you'll see how stacking breath with movement, touch, or sound leverages your physiology for lasting ease—laying the path for the next tools in your anxiety management kit (Miranda, 2023; Ma et al., 2024).

Resonant Breathing Practice

Now that you understand why longer exhales bring calm by activating your vagal brake, it's time to put this knowledge into practice. Resonant breathing gives you a hands-on tool to regulate your nervous system right where you are. This practice is about more than moving air—you're inviting both body and mind to enter a state of steady, supported ease (Gerritsen & Band, 2018; Magnon et al., 2021).

Setup

Find a position that feels safe and comfortable. You can lie down on your back with knees bent, feet flat, and a cushion under your hips to give your diaphragm extra space. If lying down makes your breath shallow or leaves you dizzy, prop yourself up at a gentle angle with pillows behind your back and knees. Sitting is just as helpful for many people: choose a chair with your feet flat on the ground, sitting forward so your back stays long and open.

Let your hands act as friendly guides—not measuring devices. Place one palm on your upper chest, the other on your belly, just below your ribs. When you inhale, feel for movement under your lower hand. If you notice your chest rising more, it's simply information about your current habit, not a mistake. Inhaling through your nose, let your belly expand gently under your hand. If you're in a bigger body or pregnancy, open your knees wider or rest your arms wherever comfort comes easily.

Soften your jaw by letting your back teeth separate slightly, unhinging any tension. Rest your tongue on the roof of your mouth just behind your front teeth. Let your gaze soften, closing your eyes if it feels safe or turning your focus downward. These tweaks nudge your body toward a sense of safety and make each breath smoother, supporting vagal activity and relaxation (Gerritsen & Band, 2018).

Timing

Aim for a soft, even inhale through the nose over four or five seconds. It may help to silently count "one, two, three, four" as you fill up, feeling your lower ribs widen a touch. Then exhale slowly for six or seven seconds, keeping your lips closed or barely parted. Imagine fogging up a delicate mirror or blowing up an almost-full balloon—you want the outward breath quiet and easy. This approach brings most people close to five or six breaths per minute, a range shown to lift heart rate variability and help balance both branches of your nervous system (Magnon et al., 2021).

If counting seconds feels tense, try humming or sighing quietly on your out-breath. Let the sound be your guide for how long to exhale. Free apps for paced breathing can also offer a gentle visual or audio cue.

Notice what feels kindest to your body. If the suggested pace feels strained, shorten your inhale and exhale by a second or two, or remove the count entirely. If you find after a handful of rounds that your out-breath could last a little longer, bump it up by a second. The aim is always comfort—never force.

Diaphragmatic, low, slow breaths are what help unlock the soothing effects (Gerritsen & Band, 2018).

Duration

Set a timer for five minutes—the sweet spot for most beginners. Consistent, brief practice does far more to train your system than occasional, long sessions. Try two five-minute sessions daily if you can: once in the morning, once at night. Settle in, start your timer, then let yourself relax into the rhythm without clock-watching (Magnon et al., 2021).

If you notice dizziness, tingling, chest tightness, or a panicky feeling, stop immediately. Return to normal breathing, open your eyes, and orient yourself by noticing things around you. Resume with fewer minutes, slower breaths, or upright posture. Even two minutes is valuable. You're in charge—moving gently and pausing when needed is a sign of attunement, not failure.

Checkpoints

Before you begin, ask yourself how calm you feel on a scale from zero to ten. Take this number again afterwards. Many people notice a two- or three-point drop in their anxiety, but some changes are subtle—a warmer sensation in your fingers, jaw released, vision softening, or a sense of spreading warmth as stress releases its grip (Magnon et al., 2021).

Keep a small journal or notepad nearby and jot one or two lines after each session: maybe, "Humming made it easier" or "Shorter exhale felt better today." Over time, these notes help you personalize your practice. This is about discovery, not performance, and every session teaches you something about your body's needs.

Sometimes, even a gentle breath practice can stir discomfort or memories. Should anything feel wrong, open your eyes, look around, name objects in the room, and skip the exercise if needed. There's no requirement to push through. Safety is the anchor; you can always return to another calming tool from your toolkit. Some days you might stick with just a couple of minutes or keep your eyes open. Flexibility means you're honoring your own healing rhythm.

Resonant breathing offers a reliable foundation for nervous system health, easing anxiety with each cycle. With time, your system will adapt, making this technique an accessible pillar for daily self-care (Gerritsen & Band, 2018; Magnon et al., 2021). For those moments when stress arrives fast and sharp, you'll find the next section's physiological sigh provides an even quicker reset.

Physiological Sigh Technique

This exercise plays a central role in the book's mission to equip you with rapid, science-based strategies for managing anxiety. You've learned how longer exhales shift your body toward calm—now it's time for hands-on practice with the physiological sigh, a technique shown to quickly downshift autonomic arousal and improve mood (Balban et al., 2023; Leggett, 2023). By guiding your breath through a two-part inhale and an extra-long exhale, you use your physiology as a direct lever for nervous system reset. This exercise bridges theory and daily life: whether you're parked before a big meeting or steadying yourself after a shock, it helps you flip the internal switch from tense to settled within moments.

Physiological Sigh

Target areas: Chest, diaphragm, ribcage, upper respiratory muscles

Difficulty: Beginner

Duration: 1–2 minutes (or up to 5 minutes if using as a full reset)

Steps:

Find a safe, comfortable seat with both feet grounded. Sit upright but allow your belly to soften.

Inhale gently through your nose until your lungs feel about three-quarters full—let your lower ribs and sides expand, keeping shoulders relaxed.

Without exhaling, take a quick, short second inhale through your nose—this "top-up" puff is small, just enough to lift the upper chest slightly and further open the air sacs.

Exhale very slowly and fully through pursed lips, as if cooling hot soup. Let the exhale extend naturally and imagine tension melting away with the out-breath.

At the end of the exhale, pause briefly without holding your breath. Notice any softening in your face, mouth, and jaw.

Repeat for 3–5 cycles. Each cycle takes roughly 10–15 seconds. If you sense clear relief earlier (shoulders dropping, jaw unclenching, warmth spreading), you may stop sooner.

Insert a neutral nose breath between cycles to prevent overbreathing and check in on comfort. Modifications:

- If you become lightheaded, stop immediately, return to regular gentle nose breathing, and remain seated until steady.
- Those with asthma or respiratory sensitivity should keep inhales gentle and skip forced exhales. When in doubt, seek medical guidance.

Body Awareness Tips:

- Emphasize expanding your torso outward and upward during inhales, then allow your body to relax and settle with each exhale.
- Keep your neck, jaw, and shoulders loose throughout; avoid lifting shoulders during the top-up inhale.
- Monitor for signs of overexertion: tingling, dizziness, breath hunger—use these as cues to scale back or substitute with softer breathing methods.

Common Mistakes to Avoid:

- Forcing large or fast inhales (which can trigger breathlessness)
- Overemphasizing the exhale to the point of strain
- Rushing transitions between steps rather than allowing natural, unforced rhythm

Why It Matters:

- This method interrupts the worry–body tension spiral by flattening your physiological arousal through direct shifts in lung inflation and vagal tone (Balban et al., 2023; Leggett, 2023).

- The slow, controlled exhale signals safety to your brain, rapidly lowering heart rate and anxiety intensity so you can move forward with more clarity.
- Practicing 3–5 reps as needed fits even in tight windows—before a call, after startling news, or mid-worry loop. No special equipment, no need to leave your chair, just your attention and breath.

In the next section, you'll learn how to enhance these calming effects even further by adding voiced exhales and humming—a simple layer that boosts vagal feedback and brings extra warmth and resonance into your practice.

Humming for Vagal Vibration

The sensation of humming offers a soothing anchor for the nervous system, layering resonance and gentle sound over the calming breathwork you have just practiced. After learning how to work with breath as an immediate reset through physiological sighs, embracing voiced exhales brings in another dimension: vibration. The simple act of humming sends a soft buzz up through your chest, throat, and face, which the vagus nerve picks up along its pathway. This vibratory feedback not only signals your body to downshift but also sets up your face and voice for social engagement, smoothing your transition into interactions or helping unwind tension before rest (Myers, 2025; Vagus Nerve | Psychology Today, n.d.).

Choose a Note: Gentle hum on exhale for 10–20 breaths

Think of humming as a quiet purr rather than a song. There's no need to aim for musicality or volume—just set your breath at ease. Start by taking a gentle inhale through your nose, then let the air flow out as you softly hum. Try aiming for a low-to-mid pitch; most people find it less straining and more pleasant. Pay attention to how your throat feels. If you notice tightness or any discomfort, lower your pitch and reduce how much air you push out until the sound feels easy and effortless again. The end goal is comfort, not performance. Your hum may be barely audible or just felt as a faint vibration inside your mouth and chest—this is perfectly fine. Every hum, no matter how quiet, works to stimulate your vagal pathways (Myers, 2025).

Facial Resonance: Feel vibration in lips, nose, and throat

As you hum, rest your fingertips gently on your lips or across the bridge of your nose. Notice the subtle tingling or buzz beneath your fingers. If you sense little or no vibration, experiment by rounding your lips or letting your jaw relax slightly open. Smile softly or shift your hum a notch higher or lower until you find a spot that makes your face tingle.

Imagine the sound spreading into the "mask" area encompassing your cheeks, upper lip, and nose. Keeping awareness in these spots draws your mind away from anxious spirals and anchors you firmly in the present, encouraging a feeling of safety. Each hum becomes a way to signal safety right through your facial muscles—a powerful part of the body's own reassurance system (Vagus Nerve | Psychology Today, n.d.; Myers, 2025).

Add Hands: One hand on sternum to amplify soothing

For another layer of comfort, place your palm gently over your breastbone. Let your hand rest there while you hum, feeling each vibration echo into your chest with every exhale. You don't need to press hard—just enough to feel settled. The warmth and stability of your palm combine with the internal resonance from humming, creating a deeper sense of being held. Breathe in slowly for about 4 seconds, then hum on your exhale for 6–7 seconds, letting the rhythm guide you into steadiness. It can help to imagine your hand acting like a cozy weight, easing your heart rate and inviting your body into calm (Myers, 2025; Vagus Nerve | Psychology Today, n.d.).

Social Cue Boost: Soft smile and relaxed eyes to engage ventral vagal

Facial expressions are a direct line to your nervous system's feelings of safety or threat. As you continue humming, let the corners of your mouth lift slightly in a half-smile and allow your eyes to soften. Take in more of your surroundings with your peripheral vision. On each exhale, silently affirm to yourself, 'I'm safe enough now' or 'This moment is okay.' Pairing this gentle smile and relaxed gaze with humming boosts the vagus nerve's social engagement branch, making your voice sound warmer and your body language more welcoming. Using these cues even for a few minutes before connecting with others, whether in person or virtually, can lower jaw tension, steady your breathing, and create a ripple of calm throughout your system (Myers, 2025; Vagus Nerve | Psychology Today, n.d.).

Try stacking these elements together for a complete two- to three-minute nervous system reset. Start with two minutes of resonant breathing as learned earlier, follow with three slow physiological sighs, then ease into ten humming exhales, layering your palm on your chest, fingertips on your face, and a soft smile. This micro-routine fits easily before meetings, gatherings, bedtime, or any time you want to arrive grounded. Give yourself permission to play with the practice—hum quietly during a walk, in the car, or tucked away in a quiet corner. If your throat grows tired or humming causes strain, pause, sip water, and resume with a lighter touch. Building confidence takes time; if self-consciousness rises, start alone and let the simplicity of the sound remind you that safety can be summoned anywhere, anytime (Myers, 2025; Vagus Nerve | Psychology Today, n.d.).

Chapter 5

COLD, TOUCH, AND SOUND: NON-INVASIVE VNS YOU CAN FEEL

Imagine two people caught in the grip of sudden anxiety. One battles on with sheer willpower, pushing through the discomfort, but remains tense and wired long after the moment passes. The other takes a different approach: they splash cool water on their cheeks, place a hand gently over their heart, and hum along to a comforting song. Within minutes, their racing mind slows, and calm settles in like a soothing balm. This contrast reveals something crucial — it's not about toughness or determination, but rather how skillfully the body's natural calming systems are engaged to send signals of safety to the brain and nervous system.

This chapter will guide you through using cold, touch, and sound as simple, non-invasive ways to activate the vagus nerve, the body's built-in pathway to ease stress quickly.

Starting with gentle exposure to safe cold sensations that you can try immediately, you'll learn how these sensory cues work together to quiet anxiety and foster steady calm. Each method builds on the last, offering practical tools that fit into everyday life and empower you to regain balance when anxiety strikes without struggle or excessive effort.

Brief Cold Exposure Basics

You don't have to plunge into an ice bath or stand shivering in a frozen shower to engage your vagus nerve with cold. Instead, brief exposure to cool temperatures on the face and neck, done safely and gently, can send calming signals through your body—no extreme discomfort required (Jungmann et al., 2018; Richer et al., 2022). For many, this makes vagal toning through cold accessible and inviting, even if past experiences with the cold felt overwhelming.

Start with "Face Dunk Lite" by using either cool tap water or a wrapped gel pack for just half a minute. The key areas are the cheekbones and the orbital bone just under your eyes.

Feel along your face where your cheekbones curve out and your fingers naturally sit under your eyes—that's the zone to target. These spots are loaded with nerves linked to the trigeminal-facial-vagal pathway. When you apply coolness here, those nerves carry messages straight to your brainstem that it's safe to slow down heart rate and deepen your breath, echoing ancient dive reflexes that help mammals conserve energy underwater (Jungmann et al., 2018; Richer et al., 2022).

Choose the option that fits your needs. Either splash cool tap water onto your cheeks using cupped hands for 30–60 seconds, or wrap a soft kitchen towel around a gel ice pack and rest it lightly across both cheeks. You should feel a refreshing coolness—not biting cold. If you flinch or tense up, the temperature is too strong. After 30 seconds, place one hand on your chest. Notice the beat of your heart and see if your breathing has slowed or feels more comfortable. This feedback builds trust in the technique and helps you sense subtle changes from session to session. If you enjoy gentle tactile sensations, remember that next you'll learn how touch alone, even without cold, can be just as soothing—a simple hand on the cheek or gentle pressure can offer similar nervous system support.

The same calm pathway works through the sides of your neck, but safety is crucial. Never place cold directly over the front of your throat. Sit comfortably and find the sternocleidomastoid muscle—the firm, rope-like band running from behind your ear to your collarbone. Gently turn your head and feel this muscle tighten under your fingertips. Take a cool, damp washcloth or wrap a gel pack in a towel, then rest it along one side of this muscle for no longer than 10–20 seconds. Stay off the windpipe and stick to the lateral neck area. Baroreceptors near the carotid artery detect cooling and help regulate blood pressure and heart rate, nudging your body toward a calmer baseline (Jungmann et al., 2018). Because some people may get lightheaded with neck cooling, always start while sitting, then rise slowly after a short pause. If you notice any dizziness, skip repeating on the other side and return to cheek cooling or breathing techniques instead. For many, the soft chill paired with the feeling of gentle contact brings reassurance—a hint of what you'll explore further with touch-based self-soothing practices.

If you prefer whole-body approaches, use your regular shower time to add a gentle contrast. Turn down the temperature for just 10–30 seconds at the end of a warm shower. Aim the cooler water first at your upper back and shoulders, letting it run gradually down your arms and legs. Wait until you hear yourself take a small gasp, then settle into steady breaths within a breath or two. There's no need to aim for icy cold—just enough briskness to wake up your skin, not punish it. Avoid the face and head unless you already feel confident. Finish with a blast of warm water, or step out and towel off briskly, letting friction and movement restore warmth. Over several days, what once felt sharp will become friendlier, as your nervous system adapts and your stress response softens with practice (Jungmann et al., 2018).

Keep in mind the safest way to benefit from cold is through short exposures. Watch carefully for warning signs: stop immediately if you experience chest pain, tightness, breath restriction that doesn't resolve quickly, strong shivering lasting beyond 30 seconds after warming up, or any sense of panic. Those with cardiovascular issues, Raynaud's, or thyroid problems should check with a clinician before trying cold practices. Let comfort guide you: a little bit, done often, is far more effective than rare moments of struggle or unpleasant endurance (Jungmann et al., 2018; Richer et al., 2022). And if cold simply isn't a fit for your body, remember the next sections bring more tools—gentle touch and sound-based methods ready to carry you forward toward steady calm.

Self-Soothing With Touch

Touch is a direct and accessible way to shift the body out of anxiety and into a state of calm. Gentle touch, warmth, and rhythmic movement send powerful safety signals through the nervous system, activating vagal pathways that help slow heart rate, deepen breath, and settle racing thoughts (Gerritsen & Band, 2018; Haynes et al., 2022). When cold exposure feels uncomfortably intense or impractical, self-soothing touch offers a simple alternative. These techniques aim to regulate arousal by connecting attention to sensation while providing options to adjust pressure, duration, and focus to suit each individual's comfort.

Hand on Heart: Anchoring Safety And Calm

Pressing the hand over the heart taps into mechanoreceptors beneath the skin and stimulates baroreceptors that sense gentle pressure. This action sends a calming signal to the brainstem via the vagus nerve, helping to relieve tension and slow the body's stress response. The warmth from your palm, combined with gentle weight, draws awareness inward and away from anxious scanning. Place one hand at the center-left of your chest just above the heart. Rest the other hand lightly on your belly to feel the movement of your breath. Breathe in slowly for a count of four and exhale for a count of six, letting the exhale grow softer and longer each round. Notice warmth spreading under your palm as you breathe. If it helps, quietly pair this touch with a phrase like, "Right now, I'm safe enough," though silent attention to the bodily feeling works just as well. Feel for small changes in your body—jaw muscles letting go, shoulders falling away from the ears, or a sense of softening across your chest. Use this technique anywhere—at home, in public, seated or lying down—as a discreet, grounding practice (Gerritsen & Band, 2018; Haynes et al., 2022).

Butterfly Hug: Rhythm for Integration

Bilateral stimulation through alternating left-right tapping helps organize the nervous system by engaging both sides of the brain and offering a predictably calming rhythm. Instead of tapping hard, think of light drumming or feather-touch pulses that invite rather than demand relaxation. Cross your arms so each palm rests on the opposite upper arm or collarbone. Let your fingers relax. Begin tapping gently, left then right, about once per second. Keep eyes open, focused softly on a steady point, or let them close if you feel comfortable. After ten to fifteen taps, pause. Check whether your jaw feels looser, your shoulders have dropped, or your breath has deepened. If all feels steady, continue for another set. If you notice agitation rising, stop and choose another soothing method, such as placing a hand on your heart or slow breathing. This process trains the body to respond to rhythm as a cue for settling, building flexibility in handling elevated arousal (Haynes et al., 2022).

Vagal Stroke: Tracing Ease Along the Neck

The vagus nerve passes close to the surface just below the ear along the large neck muscle known as the sternocleidomastoid. Gentle stroking here provides sensory input that encourages vagal activation without needing pressure or force. Using two fingertips, start just under the ear lobe and very lightly trace a path down and forward toward the collarbone, following the edge of the neck muscle but staying beside—not over—the windpipe. Match each stroke to an easy, slow exhale, repeating five to eight times on each side. Pause after finishing one side and check for subtle shifts—a warming sensation, a softening of the throat, or the chest easing open. If any area feels tight or sore, lighten your touch further or switch to a different side. Readers sensitive to neck touch can skip this technique altogether and focus on the jaw or hands instead (Gerritsen & Band, 2018).

Jaw Release: Unlocking Tension at the Hinge

Jaw tension is one of the most common ways the body reacts to anxiety, tightening the masseter and temporalis muscles and triggering feedback signals that keep the system on high alert. Releasing this area interrupts the cycle and invites the trigeminal-vagal pathways to settle. Find the hinge points just in front of each ear where the jaw opens and closes.

Using your fingertips, draw small, slow circles at these points, then sweep down toward the chin and back up. Combine the jaw massage with a tongue drop: rest the tip of your tongue behind your lower teeth, letting the base of your tongue drop completely. This move allows the jaw to unclench naturally and reduces facial holding. Complete the sequence with three relaxed yawns or a few seconds of soft humming, letting the vibration further signal safety to your system. Feel for warmth in your cheeks, a sense of looseness in your jaw, and easier movement in your neck. For those who find touch overstimulating, a simple yawn alone still activates quieting pathways (Gerritsen & Band, 2018; Haynes et al., 2022).

Each of these practices adapts easily to suit different needs. In public, hand-on-heart may be used quietly, while in private, jaw release or gentle neck strokes offer more thorough settling. Eyes can remain open during a butterfly hug if closing them feels unsafe. Layering touch with breath or sound builds stronger effects: humming softly after a jaw release, combining neck strokes with a long exhale, or pairing hand-on-heart with a repeated calming phrase. Every gesture offers a moment to check in and shape the body's response. These tactile strategies, paired with mindful breathing, create a toolkit that supports nervous system balance wherever you are (Gerritsen & Band, 2018; Haynes et al., 2022).

Acoustic Pathways to Calm

With cold and touch established as immediate vagal activators, sound offers a third pathway—one that works through both external listening and internal vibration to signal safety and lengthen your exhale. Adding acoustic input builds on the somatic anchors you've already practiced, moving from hands-on comfort to influences that flow through your ears, voice, and body. This foundation prepares you to layer additional techniques as you become more comfortable, but start by focusing on mastering individual options before combining them.

Sound engages the vagus nerve through two routes: one is the listening pathway, where the ear picks up reassuring signals in music or voices; the other is the vibrational pathway, which is activated when you create sound with your own vocal cords. These channels work directly on the ventral branch of the vagus, the system's social engagement circuit that tells your body it's safe to open, connect, and rest (vagus, schmagus! — waning crescent wellness, 2025; Fooks & Niebuhr, 2024).

Prosody is the melodic, rhythmic quality of speech—the rise and fall, warmth, and friendly tone that sets calm people apart from those who sound flat or harsh. When you listen to prosodic voices, your body picks up subtle cues of safety through the auditory nerve, sending signals to the ventral vagal network. Friendly podcasts, meditations led by gentle speakers, audiobooks read by soothing narrators, and even certain nature documentaries create this effect. Voices that are monotone, sharp, or rushed can nudge your nervous system toward stress instead of ease. If you're alone, reading aloud in a soft, warm tone helps trigger this response for yourself. You don't need performance skills—a simple, mindful delivery is what matters. Reading poetry, affirmations, or comforting stories out loud lets you feel the calming rhythm while also hearing it.

Remember from Chapter 2 that prosody—the melodic quality of voice—directly influences ventral vagal tone, the branch responsible for social engagement and calm. The acoustic strategies you're learning here leverage that biology (Fooks & Niebuhr, 2024; vagus, schmagus! — waning crescent wellness, 2025).

The qualities of the music you choose make a real difference for your nervous system. Aim for slow tempos between 60 and 80 beats per minute (BPM), which mirrors the resting human heart rate, supporting breath regulation and natural calm. Volume should stay at 60–70 decibels, about as loud as a quiet conversation or soft background radio—never so high you can't hear someone speaking nearby. Music that's too loud or too fast can ramp up alertness rather than settle it (Fooks & Niebuhr, 2024). Pick tracks you know by heart. Familiarity lowers mental effort and reduces the risk of unexpected emotional spikes, so your brain doesn't have to scan for new information. A "calm playlist" with five to ten peaceful songs is a great tool. Avoid pieces with sudden dynamic shifts or lyrics that directly relate to stressful experiences. Test your playlist in different moments and update it as needed—old favourites often work best for winding down after a tense day.

In public or uncertain environments, sticking both earbuds in can actually increase jitteriness for some. When both ears are blocked, your nervous system may become hyper-alert, fearing it can't monitor threats. One solution is "safe buds": use a single earbud or headphones with transparency mode, which allows ambient sounds to filter through. Nature sounds, or instrumental music, create less distraction than words when you're trying to stay present. Keep your head up, glance around gently, and check how you feel. Try out this setup first in a place where you already feel comfortable, then branch out gradually. Always notice if using headphones increases tension—in that case, return to an open-ear option and focus on breath or touch instead (vagus, schmagus! — waning crescent wellness, 2025).

Singing or chanting delivers two benefits at once. First, you naturally stretch out your exhale, which puts the brakes on stress signals, as described earlier in this book. Second, vibration from vocalizing stimulates vagal pathways along your throat, chest, and face—helpful even if you're not musically trained. Hum softly on each out-breath for four to six seconds, paying attention to sensations in your lips, chin, jaw, and sternum. Complete three to five rounds, letting your breath settle between each one. Simple sounds like "mmm," "ohm," or a favourite syllable work well, centring your awareness on how vibration feels rather than what the sound "should" be. Signs you're getting benefits could include feeling your heart slow, jaw muscles loosen, or breathing deepen. There's no pressure to get it right every time—just noticing what shifts helps guide your next attempt (Fooks & Niebuhr, 2024; vagus, schmagus! — waning crescent wellness, 2025).

If any technique here leaves you more wired or uncomfortable, stop and try a gentler approach. Sound choices are personal and context-dependent. Your experience will shift day to day. Once you're comfortable with these practices, you'll combine them with cold and touch techniques to amplify your results.

Stacking Sensations for Stability

You now know how sounds like humming, singing, and prosodic voices can support calm, with attention to details such as volume and tone for comfort. Many readers find these sound techniques gentle on the system, especially when using melodic music or quiet vocalizations around 60–70 decibels (Hamilton, 2025). Building on this, combining two sensory approaches—when done gradually—can further tip the nervous system toward safety without overwhelming it. Think of this as layering smaller inputs, letting your body recognize stability before introducing anything new.

A simple place to start is the combination of humming and a hand over the heart. This pairing combines vibration and warmth, creating a feedback loop between touch and sound. Place your palm flat over your breastbone, with just enough pressure to feel the movement under your skin. Hum any pitch that feels natural, letting the vibration travel from your lips through your chest wall and into your hand. Repeat two full humming exhales, then pause for one gentle recovery breath—quiet and unforced—to let the sensation settle.

Track for signs that your system is downshifting: do your shoulders soften, does your throat feel more open, or does your breath deepen? If you don't notice much change in your first round, keep at it for three or four cycles. Your body may respond better on the second or third cycle as it recognizes this pattern (Hamilton, 2025). If you want extra grounding, try bringing awareness to the skin temperature or heartbeat beneath your hand. There's no need to push for longer or louder hums; trust what feels comfortable in the moment.

When mental chatter runs high and thought loops won't stop, a cool compress paired with slow exhale steps in as a targeted reset. Here, you're adding cold to the face with gentle breathwork to get two calming effects at once. Use a soft gel pack or a damp washcloth cooled in the fridge—not ice-cold—and wrap it so there's no shock against your skin. Press it lightly against your cheeks for 20–30 seconds, right where you'd place blush, near the trigeminal nerve area. As you hold it there, breathe in for four counts, out for six, keeping your exhalation long and easy. The cool on your cheeks signals your brain to slow heart rate (the dive reflex), while your prolonged exhale nudges the vagal brake—together they interrupt anxiety's engine (Can, 2025; Hamilton, 2025). When you remove the compress, continue two more slow breaths. Stop right away if you shiver, tense up, or feel lightheaded; switch back to a simpler grounding method until balance returns. Only repeat the whole sequence once per session—more isn't always better. Adjust temperature and pressure as needed—your sense of safety is the most reliable guide here.

Some days, restlessness shows up as an urge to move or fidget. Music with gentle rocking offers both sensory and motor input—a solid choice when sitting still feels impossible. Sit upright with feet planted or stand hip-width apart, then choose a familiar song with a steady rhythm (ideally 60–80 beats per minute, matching a relaxed heart rate) (Hamilton, 2025). Begin swaying or rocking side to side in time with the music. Make each movement small and stable, only a few inches in either direction. You might close your eyes or rest your gaze softly on a fixed spot to settle your vision. This double soothing—predictable sound with regular motion—tells multiple sensory systems there's no threat, dimming alarm signals in the brainstem (Hamilton, 2025). After a minute, pause all movement and take two quiet breaths to help your body register the shift. If dizziness or discomfort sneaks in, stay still and focus on your breath until you feel steady again. Try this practice during evenings at home, or whenever you sense agitation building.

Tuning your routine always starts with adding only one new element at a time. If you're comfortable humming, layer in the hand-on-heart and keep everything else unchanged.

Check in after one or two minutes—note which sensations feel grounding and how strong or mild your relief is. A simple log can help: jot down the method, duration, and a quick number from 1 (no effect or worse) to 5 (big relief). Marking a 3 as success, not perfection, helps build confidence in your results. If a technique feels too intense—tightening, spinning thoughts, shallow breaths—immediately peel back the newest layer and return to the last thing that felt safe. That's feedback, not failure: your system is giving you guidance you can trust (Can, 2025; Hamilton, 2025).

Every person finds their own pace—you're allowed to skip or modify any part based on what feels right. Pay attention to clear cues: vibration in the lips, warmth under your palm, coolness across your cheeks, the sway in your hips. These are all signs you're engaging your body's calming wires—in ways that fit you best.

Training your nervous system happens through regular, gentle practice. Try choosing one single-modality tool and one paired stack to use daily this week. Keep routines short and uncomplicated—a few easy cycles every morning or before bed makes a bigger impact than chasing the perfect sequence or pushing limits. Consistency, not complexity, builds real-life resilience (Hamilton, 2025; Can, 2025). Your own notes and numbers hold more value than any formula found elsewhere. Day by day, you'll get better at knowing which combination helps you return to steady ground.

Chapter 6

MINDFUL ATTENTION AND GENTLE MOVEMENT

Maya used to feel trapped by the sensory overload of grocery stores: harsh fluorescent lights, constant beeping of scanners, and the crush of people in narrow aisles. Her body tensed automatically, heart pounding and shoulders raised as if bracing for impact. One Saturday, just moments from leaving her full cart behind, she recalled a simple technique from her therapist. She paused and scanned her surroundings for five things that felt neutral or pleasant. She noticed the vibrant green apples stacked neatly, the gentle smile from the cashier, the quiet hum of the refrigerators, the cool touch of the metal cart handle under her fingers, and the bright label on her favourite tea. Each item she named softly to herself helped slow her breath and ground her feet on the floor. That small shift was enough to turn down her nervous system's red alert toward a sense of safety and calm.

This chapter invites you to explore the same mindful attention and gentle movement that brought Maya relief. You'll begin with a straightforward orienting practice for any place and moment. By gently tuning into your environment through your senses and connecting with subtle bodily support, you can create a steady base of calm amid everyday challenges. These methods offer practical ways to ease tension, refocus your mind, and invite your nervous system into relaxation even during busy or stressful times.

Through mindful noticing and simple movements, you'll build tools to help yourself feel safe, steady, and present again.

Orienting to Safety: A Guided Practice for Everyday Calm

Anxiety often locks attention onto possible threats, cycling endlessly for signs of danger. Orienting shifts this habit by inviting the nervous system to register safety cues right where you are. When you pause to notice your environment and label neutral or pleasant details, you send calming signals to your brainstem, breaking the loop of hypervigilance and allowing a natural downshift toward calm (Porges, 2022; Sutton, 2023). This quick practice lays the groundwork for more advanced techniques by establishing a baseline of steady comfort you can return to anytime.

Look and Name

Pause wherever you are—at the grocery store, in your kitchen, or waiting for a meeting to start.

Gently let your gaze wander around the space. Notice textures, shapes, and colors in your surroundings.

Pick out five things that feel neutral or pleasant. These could be the soft green of a houseplant, the smooth pattern on a mug, a shaft of light across the floor, or the geometric shape of a ceiling tile. Avoid focusing on objects that make you tense or upset.

For each item, silently or softly whisper its name to yourself: "Green plant," "Blue mug," "Light through window." Naming engages the part of the brain responsible for problem-solving (the prefrontal cortex), which helps quiet the alarm center (the amygdala) (Sutton, 2023).

After naming each item, pause for one full breath. Notice if anything softens in your body—a slight release in the jaw, less clenching in your shoulders, or a melting sensation behind your eyes. Even the smallest micro-release signals that the exercise is working, as your nervous system shifts from defense to calm (Kolacz et al., 2020b; Porges, 2022). If five feels like too much, start with three. If saying words aloud is uncomfortable, just think them. Maya, who found herself overwhelmed in the canned goods aisle, started by picking out only two: "Red label," "Silver shelf." She whispered these to herself and felt her chest ease a little. You might do the same during a tense family dinner or in a public restroom between meetings.

Expand Hearing

After looking, bring your awareness to sounds. Start with distant noises—the hum of an air conditioner, passing cars, a bird outside. Let these create a sense of openness and space that counters tunnel vision. Next, listen for nearby sounds: your own breathing, the shuffle of your shoes, a distant conversation. Don't attach stories or judgments to these sounds. Instead, notice their presence as pure sensation.

Tell yourself, "I'm just listening."If anxious thoughts pop up, such as "That siren means trouble," it's okay. Let the thought pass and gently return to the raw sound itself. Non-judgmental listening reassures the autonomic nervous system that it's safe to monitor without needing to defend (Porges, 2022; Sutton, 2023).

Feel Support

Now, guide your focus to physical support. Press your feet lightly into the floor. Notice sensations: pressure, warmth, coolness, or softness. Shift awareness to your sit bones or your back, making contact with a chair. Allow a 5–10% softening—just enough so your muscles let go of some bracing, but you stay upright. Repeat quietly in your mind: "Supported here, supported now."Linking gentle self-talk with bodily sensation combines cognitive comfort with physical reassurance, reassuring your nervous system that support is available in this moment (Sutton, 2023). Feel the seat holding your weight, or your hands resting against your thighs, as real-time anchors of safety. In busy environments, like buses or crowded waiting rooms, this simple act grounds you even more effectively than trying to relax all at once.

Completion Breath

Seal the practice with one intentional exhale. Purse your lips slightly, as if cooling soup. Breathe out slowly for six to eight seconds. As you exhale, picture your shoulders gliding down and back just a little—no force, just gravity. At the end of the exhale, pause for a second or two before letting the next inhale arrive naturally.

This single slow breath signals to your nervous system that the threat has passed. The brief pause after exhaling gives the vagal brake—the body's built-in relaxation switch—time to activate fully (Sutton, 2023; Porges, 2022).

Whether you're standing in line, sitting at your desk, or lying down after a long day, you can practice this in almost any position. Adjust steps as needed: try just the hearing section if sights are overwhelming, or shorten to three items if time is tight. Whisper labels or say them quietly in your mind if privacy is needed.

Building Confidence With Each Round

Hypervigilance is not a personal flaw; it's a protective brain response that has kept you safe before (Porges, 2022).

Shifting focus takes practice, and noticing even one item or sound counts as a win. Track your sense of calm before and after with a simple 0–10 rating. Pause or stop whenever you need to. If orienting to your environment increases anxiety, anchor in an inner resource—your breath, the feel of your hand over your heart, or the pressure of your feet.

As you become familiar with orienting, this new sense of safety becomes your steady base. Soon, you'll learn how to gently move your attention between comfort and discomfort, using pendulation and titration to build your capacity for calm without getting overwhelmed.

Pendulation and Titration Basics

Now that you can anchor yourself in the present moment using sensory awareness, you're ready to work with what's happening inside your body. This next step is about guiding your attention between comfort and discomfort in ways that increase your capacity for sensation without tipping into overwhelm. The practices of pendulation and titration teach you how to 'dose' each somatic experience, creating just the right challenge for your nervous system so it keeps learning rather than locking up (Nicholson et al., 2025; Murraysville, 2025).

Pendulation means gently moving your attention back and forth between a safe, comfortable sensation—a resource—and an area with some tension or discomfort. A resource could be warmth in your hands, the solid support of a chair under you, or a feeling of calm somewhere in your body.

Always find your resource first. For example, maybe you notice your belly feels settled, or your hands are warm. Once you've anchored there, let your focus shift for just 5-10 seconds to mild discomfort, such as tightness in your chest or a prickly feeling in your legs. Return to your resource for 20-30 seconds, letting ease or stability spread. The goal isn't to erase discomfort but to observe changes: does tension lessen even slightly? Does the discomfort move, soften, or become clearer? Each round builds the message that sensations rise and fall, helping your brain learn they're temporary and manageable (Nicholson et al., 2025; Murraysville, 2025).

Titration takes this idea further by breaking down what you feel into the smallest sips your system can handle. Think of it as giving the nervous system just a taste, not the whole meal. Rate any sensation on a scale from 0 (nothing) to 10 (unbearable distress). Aim for a level of 3 or 4—noticeable but not overwhelming, a place where you remain curious and alert. If tuning in to your whole body feels like too much, shrink it: pay attention only to your left hand, or even one finger. If taking a deep breath feels too intense, try just a gentle inhale. Revisiting a stressful memory? Zoom in on a neutral part, like the color of a wall or a sound in the background. These small doses keep you within your window of tolerance, where your system can process new information without reverting to old patterns (Nicholson et al., 2025). Settling cues—like letting out a slow sigh, softening your gaze, or pressing your feet into the floor—signal to your body that it's safe to rest after exploring something new. They mark the end of each dose, telling your nervous system that you're finished for now.

Staying within the window of tolerance is your main safety compass during all somatic practices. You learned about this green-yellow-red system earlier when discussing vagal tone: green means regulated, yellow is a warning, red signals overload. Watch for clues you might be edging toward red—your breath catches, your mind races, you feel heavy, fidgety, numb, or far away. If any of these show up, it's just information: instead of pushing through, return to your resource immediately. Spend 30-60 seconds there. Notice shifts—like breath smoothing, shoulders loosening, or thoughts getting quieter—before deciding whether to continue or stop for the day. Progress in these practices comes from staying present and connected, not toughing it out or forcing change. Every time you catch yourself drifting out of the window and come back safely, you strengthen self-awareness and trust in your body (Nicholson et al., 2025; Murraysville, 2025).

Less is more when working with the nervous system. Small shifts have lasting effects because your body learns more effectively from repeated, subtle signals than from big, dramatic interventions. Soften your jaw by just five percent, let your exhale last two seconds longer, or allow your shoulders to drop a fraction—all of these can spark measurable calm in as little as half a minute. In neuroscience terms, these gentle adjustments build new brain pathways (Nicholson et al., 2025). It's consistency that matters: four short pauses during the day will retrain your stress response more reliably than one marathon session. Gentle pacing is not a sign of being fragile—it's a strategic approach that honours your body's natural pace. As you bring pendulation and titration into every movement and pause in the exercises ahead, trust that small, careful steps create real and lasting change (Nicholson et al., 2025; Murraysville, 2025).

Vagal-Friendly Mobility Flow

This mobility flow is designed to gently stimulate the vagus nerve and regulate the nervous system through slow movement, breath coordination, and mindful pacing. The exercises in this section bridge knowledge from earlier chapters—highlighting the science of vagal tone and breath—with actionable steps you can use at home, in the office, or even seated on a chair. By practicing these movements with intention and attention to alignment, you'll gain safer, body-friendly tools for calming stress and cultivating resilience. These techniques require minimal space and no equipment, making them accessible regardless of lifestyle constraints, and each movement can be adapted for diverse abilities.

Neck Glide

Target areas: Lateral neck muscles, upper trapezius, cervical spine

Difficulty: Beginner Duration: 3 breaths per side Steps:

Sit or stand tall with shoulders relaxed and chin level. Without lifting your shoulder, slide your right ear toward your right shoulder until you feel a mild stretch (aim for 3–4 out of 10 on your personal stretch scale).

Inhale through the nose; exhale slowly through pursed lips, letting your left shoulder drop away from the ear.

Hold for three complete breath cycles, then return to center. Pause to notice any warmth or release, then repeat on the left side.

Modifications: If upright posture is tiring, do this while seated fully supported.

Common Mistakes: Hiking the shoulder up to meet the ear, tensing the jaw or holding your breath.

Body Awareness Tip: Keep head movements gentle; sensation should never be sharp or pinching.

Thoracic Opener

Target areas: Mid-back (thoracic spine), obliques, chest Difficulty: Beginner

Duration: 3 cycles per side Steps:

Sit on the front edge of a sturdy chair, feet flat, pelvis anchored.

Place your hands lightly on your thighs. Inhale to lengthen the spine upward.

As you exhale, rotate gently to the right from the ribcage (not the neck), keeping the pelvis steady.

Soften your gaze or focus lightly on a stable point to reduce dizziness.

At the end of the exhale, pause for 1–2 seconds.

Unwind back to center on inhale, noticing any ease or warmth; repeat for three full cycles before switching sides. Modifications: If twisting feels too strong, keep the range small or place a pillow behind your lower back for support. Common Mistakes: Over-rotating from the neck, shifting hips off the chair, and holding the breath.

Body Awareness Tip: Movement should feel smooth and comfortable, not forced or tense.

Cat–Cow Lite

Target areas: Spinal extensors and flexors, core stabilizers, mid-back

Difficulty: Beginner Duration: 6–8 slow repetitions Steps:

Start on hands and knees with wrists under shoulders and knees under hips, or sit with both hands resting on knees/thighs.

Inhale to gently arch the spine (let the heart glide forward, tailbone rises slightly, gaze soft ahead).

Exhale to round the back, drawing the navel subtly toward the spine and tucking the chin slightly.

Keep the range of motion small and deliberately slow; avoid sharp or jerky movement.

Repeat 6–8 times, pausing one beat after each exhale to notice settling.

Modifications: Stay seated if kneeling isn't accessible; focus on tilting the pelvis and opening/closing the chest while keeping the hands on the thighs.

Common Mistakes: Forcing deep arches/rounds, collapsing into shoulders, or moving too quickly.

Body Awareness Tip: Imagine the motion rippling smoothly through the mid-back rather than hinging from the lower spine.

Rocking Reset

Target areas: Low back, sacrum, abdominals, pelvic floor
Difficulty: Beginner

Duration: 30–60 seconds Steps:

Lie on your back with your knees hugged comfortably to your chest, and wrap your arms around your shins or behind your knees.

Gently rock side-to-side like a slow metronome, massaging the lower back and sacrum against the ground.

Sync the rocking motion with slow breathing—letting exhales cue a slight deepening and softening through the belly and pelvic floor.

Continue for 30–60 seconds, staying within a comfortable range; avoid pulling knees tightly or straining the neck.

If floor work isn't accessible, sit with feet on the ground, cradle the forearms around the shins, and rock very gently while keeping the neck loose.

Modifications: Place a folded blanket under the head or back for comfort; skip the floor version if mobility is limited.

Common Mistakes: Holding the breath, over-gripping knees, or rushing the rhythm.

Body Awareness Tip: Let eyes close or soften during the sway; notice any waves of relaxation moving down the spine.

By integrating these movements into your daily routine, you provide your nervous system with soothing input that supports safety and calm. Each exercise pairs mindful breath with gentle motion, echoing the underlying mechanisms identified by research linking slow, attentive movement and deliberate respiration to vagal nerve activation (Gerritsen & Band, 2018; Charles Ethan Paccione & Henrik Børsting Jacobsen, 2019). Small, consistent practice is often more effective than occasional long sessions. Feel free to build these into short breaks, morning rituals, or wind-down routines to maximize benefit without overwhelming your schedule.

In the next section, we'll guide you through a flexible body scan practice designed to deepen interoceptive awareness, offer clear opt-out options, and reinforce safety as you continue exploring holistic anxiety relief.

Body Scan With Opt-Outs

After practicing gentle neck, spine, and rocking movements paired with breath in the previous section, your body has already experienced grounding and movement. Now attention moves inward, using those same principles of safety and agency to explore sensations one region at a time. This trauma-informed body scan gives you full permission to opt out or modify steps at any moment. Instead of completing a set sequence from head to toe, the first step is always about consent: you choose where to start and which areas to skip.

You can begin your scan at any region—eyes, hands, feet, or even shoulders. The only rule is that you decide which area feels most neutral or least activating. For instance, if tension in your jaw or forehead makes starting at your head uncomfortable, choose your feet instead. Skipping regions is not failure; it's honouring your comfort and building trust with your nervous system. When skipping an area, mentally note it as "later." You are always encouraged to reevaluate another time, but there is never pressure to cover every region in one session. This approach keeps the practice within your window of tolerance and prevents overwhelm (Schuman-Olivier et al., 2020).

When observing each body part, use clear, simple words to describe what you notice. Neutral labels keep things factual and prevent anxious storytelling. Choose one to three sensation words per region, such as "warm," "cool," "tight," "soft," "pressure," or "tingling." If you notice your shoulders, simply register "heavy, warm" and continue to the next area. Suppose irritation or sadness surfaces; briefly acknowledge with a phrase like "irritation here," then gently redirect attention to the next region. Labelling sensations this way helps you treat them as information, not threats, so emotions are less likely to spiral (Schuman-Olivier et al., 2020); (Center, 2024).

Some readers feel disconnected, spacey, or overwhelmed by longer scans. If this sounds familiar, work in short sets of two to three minutes. Set a timer for predictability and safety. One round might focus on your feet and lower legs; another could focus just on your hands and forearms.

Keeping the practice brief creates a secure container. An example schedule could include a two-minute scan of feet and legs before breakfast, a two-minute scan of hands and arms after lunch, and a two-minute torso scan before bed. Several short practices add up and often work better than forcing yourself through one long session. If you sense yourself drifting, open your eyes, sit up taller, and press your feet into the floor for a quick reality check before moving on (Schuman-Olivier et al., 2020).

Closing your body scan signals completion and safety to your nervous system. To exit, open your eyes if they're closed and name three visible objects around you—a lamp, a book, a plant—followed by one sound you hear. Next, take a small sip of water, focusing on its coolness or warmth, and notice how it travels down your throat. This simple act activates vagus pathways and resets your senses. As a final step, stand and stretch for 5 to 10 seconds, or rest your palm on a cool surface. These grounding actions help shift your focus outward and signal to your system that the practice is over. You return to everyday activities with a bit more calm and presence (Schuman-Olivier et al., 2020); (Center, 2024).

Chapter 7

SNACK SENSATIONS: CURBING CRAVINGS THE SMART WAY

Since the late 1980s, doctors have helped treat severe epilepsy by using small pulse generators that deliver safe electrical signals to the vagus nerve. This approach, approved in the US in 1997, became common for epilepsy when other treatments failed. By 2005, its use had grown to treat severe depression. Continued research then led to safer, non-invasive devices, making nerve stimulation accessible beyond hospitals.

Today, adults with chronic anxiety can choose from simple, user-friendly devices that engage the body's calming system without surgery. These handheld and ear-clip devices bring proven clinical protocols into everyday life. This chapter traces the journey from early surgical implants to accessible, non-invasive options, showing how these advances make anxiety relief more affordable and practical for daily use.

From Implants to Non-Invasive Options

In the late 1980s, doctors could only use vagus nerve stimulation (VNS) for tough-to-treat epilepsy through surgery. This involved placing a small pulse generator in the chest, attached to the main vagus nerve branch in the neck. As discussed in earlier chapters, breath and touch can influence nerves; VNS devices aim for similar effects, but offer the consistency and dependability of technology. These devices do not replace hands-on methods but add extra support, backed by decades of clinical use (Afra et al., 2021).

The first VNS systems used surgical implants that delivered gentle pulses to the cervical vagus nerve (the main trunk in the neck), programmed to turn on and off in regular cycles. Imagine a tiny pacemaker, about the size of a matchbox, tucked under the skin near the collarbone. Thin wires called leads would snake up and wrap around the nerve. The system sent rhythmic signals throughout the day based on settings like pulse width (how long each zap lasts), frequency (how often), and duty cycle (on/off timing). These programming details weren't just technicalities—they became the safety net that let doctors adjust treatment to fit each patient's needs. Later, some patients noticed fewer seizures and surprising changes in mood and sleep, leading researchers to test VNS for depression as well (Badran & Austelle, 2022; Afra et al., 2021).

As engineers improved the devices, new models became smarter and longer-lasting. Doctors could program them wirelessly during clinic visits, which lowered the need for surgical tweaks or frequent battery changes. Safety features built into the hardware—such as magnetic wands for quick shut-off—helped calm worries about emergencies. Over time, programmers learned which combinations of pulse strength and timing worked best not just for controlling seizures but also for easing anxiety or depressive symptoms. These advances set the stage for home use: all the dialled-in parameters and safety research now appear in the default settings you'll see in today's consumer devices (Afra et al., 2021; Badran & Austelle, 2022).

Surgical VNS targets the vagus nerve trunk in the neck, often causing throat sensations, voice changes, or mild coughing at higher settings. In contrast, ear-based methods stimulate the auricular branch of the vagus nerve in the outer ear. This approach produces milder sensations, such as tingling or gentle warmth—like taking a side street instead of the highway. Both approaches activate your body's calming "rest and digest" system, but ear stimulation is gentler and brings fewer side effects. For those prioritizing comfort, ease of use, and predictability, auricular VNS fits smoothly into everyday self-care routines (Badran & Austelle, 2022).

As research labs began using ear electrodes to test non-surgical VNS in humans, device makers saw an opportunity. The careful protocols from clinics became easy presets in portable gadgets—no hospital gown or surgeon required. Handheld and wearable devices arrived with snap-on ear clips, soft pads, and simple controls. There was no more guesswork about how long to stimulate or how strong the current should be; built-in timers and stepwise intensity levels did the heavy lifting. Anyone could start slowly and increase as they get comfortable, using the same patience and self-listening skills learned back in Chapter 3.Battery-powered designs freed users from wall outlets and doctors' offices. Home VNS sessions shrank to five, ten, or fifteen minutes—easy windows to fit into commutes, lunch breaks, or bedtime wind-downs. Electrode pads moved from sticky adhesives to reusable snaps, making setup a breeze. This design shift matched what readers have practiced with breathing and touch: short bouts, done often, matter more than doing too much at once. Simplicity encourages steady practice, especially when anxiety makes decision-making harder (Badran & Austelle, 2022).

Quick session timers, progress-indicating lights, and gentle vibration cues keep things approachable. Users don't need medical training or a background in bioelectronics to feel confident. When setup is quick, and feedback is clear, people stick with it—even on tough days. Devices pair easily with other calming rituals. A reader can hum while using ear clips or spend a few device-supported minutes before sleep, adding gentle stimulation to the grounding and slow-breathing routines from earlier chapters. Each method becomes a building block, not a burden.

For most people at home, the ear is the easiest, safest place to start. Now that you understand the journey from operating room to kitchen table, let's explore how ear-based stimulation works in practice (Badran & Austelle, 2022; Afra et al., 2021).

Auricular VNS Demystified

Now that VNS devices have moved from hospitals to homes, this section explains what to expect when using an auricular device—where to place electrodes, what sensations to notice, session duration, and precautions. With this knowledge, you can approach your first session confidently.

Anatomical Targets: Finding the Right Spot on Your Ear

The two most common places for auricular VNS are the cymba concha and the tragus. If you gently touch your ear, the cymba concha is the upper "bowl" area closest to the opening of the ear canal, shaped like a shallow cup. It sits just above the entrance to the ear canal, inside the outer rim, and is often soft and smooth to the touch. The tragus, on the other hand, is the small flap in front of your ear canal—it's firm, moves when you press it, and partially covers the canal's opening. Both locations are believed to be innervated by the auricular branch of the vagus nerve (Badran et al., 2019). A slight shift of even 2-3 millimeters can change the sensation or effectiveness, so it's wise to mark your preferred spot with a washable marker or snap a quick phone photo for future sessions. Keeping consistent placement helps track how your body responds over time and makes each session more predictable.

Expected Sensations: What You'll Feel During Stimulation

Most people describe the feeling as a gentle, steady tingle that stays in one spot. Imagine the sensation of light static against your skin or a mild tap-tap-tap—not a harsh sting or jolt. Some experience a faint pulsing or light tapping under the electrode pad. The feeling should not be sharp, burning, or painful. If it becomes uncomfortable, lower the intensity until the sensation is calm and barely there. Research shows that even low-level sensations can be effective, so you do not need strong awareness for VNS to work (Badran et al., 2019).

It's normal for the skin under the electrode to look slightly red after removal. Mild soreness or noticeable after-tingling may linger for 5 or 10 minutes but should fade soon. If the redness lasts longer than an hour, or if there is blistering or persistent pain, take a break and check your technique. Using a skin-safe conductive gel and cleaning the area before application reduces irritation. Light touch and patient adjustment lead to the best results.

Session Duration Guidance: Timing Your Practice

Start with brief sessions—about five minutes at low intensity. Gradually increase to 10 or 15 minutes as you monitor calm, ease, or reduced tension. Some benefit from longer sessions. Keep a simple log of mood or physical shifts for personal reference.

Spacing sessions—such as one in the morning and one in the evening—prevents overuse and fatigue. Always pause or shorten a session if you notice discomfort, headache, or lightheadedness. Patterns vary, and your experience will guide your personal rhythm. There's no "right" amount—some stick with a single short daily session while others add time as comfort grows. Listening to your own response is the safest way forward (Aoyagi et al., 2024).

Safety Contraindications: Who Should Use Extra Caution

Screening yourself before starting auricular VNS is an act of care, not exclusion. Avoid using an auricular device directly over areas with broken, infected, or healing skin—

irritation and infection risk are higher with direct electrical contact. People with implanted cardiac devices, such as pacemakers or defibrillators, should not use VNS devices without their cardiologist's explicit guidance, as electrical currents could affect device function (Badran et al., 2019). If you have known metal allergies or sensitivities, check that the electrode materials will not cause skin reactions. Those who are pregnant, have a history of seizures, or live with cardiovascular conditions should consult with their healthcare provider before beginning VNS. Collaborating with your doctor ensures that the approach fits your needs and supports your well-being (Aoyagi et al., 2024).

Auricular VNS is generally safe and gentle, but every person brings unique health circumstances and personal goals. Screening is a partnership in personalized care rather than a barrier.

Once you know what to expect during auricular VNS—the locations, sensations, timing, and safety checks—you're set up for confident, meaningful practice. In the next section, you'll walk through your first device session step by step, turning these foundations into practical, hands-on experience.

Home Device Quick-Start

You've learned where to place ear electrodes, what a gentle tingle should feel like, and how long to run your first session. Now you're ready to take the leap from reading to trying, giving yourself a careful, positive start with auricular vagus nerve stimulation (VNS) in your own home. Each step below builds confidence while helping you listen closely to your body and track subtle changes over time. These early routines also help researchers gather reliable results on mood and anxiety (Ferstl et al., 2021; Lai et al., 2025).

Baseline Note: Record Mood and Heart Rate

Before touching your device, pause for a baseline check-in. Grab a notepad or open an app to jot down a quick snapshot of your state. Give your anxiety, mood, or stress a rating between 0 and 10—higher numbers mean you're more tense or anxious, and lower numbers mean you're calm. In just one line, describe your physical state too: "Shoulders tight, breathing shallow," or maybe, "Legs restless, mind racing." If you have a wearable that measures heart rate or HRV, note those numbers. If not, rest two fingers lightly on your wrist or side of your neck, set a timer for 60 seconds, and count your pulse beats. Write it down. Now, add a simple intention for this session: "Ease bedtime nerves" or "Help my Sunday jitters before family dinner." This short ritual grounds the session, turning a technical task into something personal and meaningful (Ferstl et al., 2021).

Intensity Ladder: Start Low, Rise Carefully

Now, pick up your VNS device. Make sure everything is clean and dry, and place the electrode as you learned—usually in your ear's concha or tragus area. Most devices start at zero or the lowest setting. Begin here, and press 'start.' For the first 30-60 seconds, you might not feel anything. That's normal. Wait, relax your hand, and let the sensation build slowly. If nothing happens after a full minute, increase the intensity by just one step. Pause again. You're looking for a steady, comfortable tingle—a soft buzz or gentle tap beneath the electrode, never sharp or burning. Stop increasing once you reach this level. More isn't better; comfort means your nervous system will trust and adapt. Some days, your skin may be more sensitive than others. Sleep, hydration, hormones, and even stress can change how strong sensations feel. Always respect these shifts (Ferstl et al., 2021; Lai et al., 2025). If today's lowest setting feels strong, trust your body and dial back.

Timing Window: Find Your Calm

Your very first session sets the tone for what comes next. Choose a quiet time when you already feel somewhat relaxed—like after breakfast, post-dinner, or just before your nightly routine. These are moments when your body naturally leans toward calm, making it easier to notice the soothing effects of VNS. Try settling into a favorite chair, silencing your phone, and letting housemates know you need ten minutes of focus. Set a timer for 5 to 10 minutes, and close your eyes if that helps you tune in. Pairing the light tingling with slow nasal breathing enhances the calming effect—inhaling for four counts, exhaling for six. You don't have to force deep breaths; just follow the gentle rhythm that feels right. Stacking relaxation techniques supports your ability to sense small shifts during practice (Ferstl et al., 2021).

Example First Session Schedule:

- Eat dinner
- Sit quietly for five minutes.
- Baseline check: mood/pulse/intention
- Place the electrode, set the device to minimum.

- Start slow breathing
- Increase intensity until you feel a gentle tingle.
- Run the device for 7 minutes.
- Finish, remove the electrode.
- Re-rate mood, log any sensations.

Post-Check: Re-rate Anxiety and Note Sensations

Right after the session, take two minutes to reflect. Rate your anxiety, mood, or stress again using the same scale. Did the number drop, rise, or stay the same? Describe any bodily shifts: Is your breathing deeper or smoother? Shoulders relaxed, jaw unclenched, or muscles still tense? Are your thoughts more transparent, slower, or unchanged? Glance at your ear—mild pinkness is fine, but soreness or angry redness means you should use less intensity or shorter sessions next time. Always log the exact intensity used so you can repeat what works or tweak what doesn't (Ferstl et al., 2021).

If you notice increased anxiety or dizziness, try shortening tomorrow's session or lowering the setting by two steps. It's normal to need some trial and error. If you felt calmer and comfortable, keep the same settings and consider scheduling your next session for about the same time each day. Consistency is key to building habits and helping your nervous system recognize the positive cues from ear-based stimulation (Lai et al., 2025).

Some people will find their rhythm quickly, while others may want extra support. There's no wrong path. If you have questions, want to personalize your practice, or face health complexities, exploring options with a professional merges science with experience, supporting you every step of the way (Lai et al., 2025).

Clinician-Guided Paths

Building on your home practice foundation, collaborating with a clinician adds an extra layer of safety and flexibility, expanding what you can do with VNS. While self-directed sessions serve many needs, some readers find it helpful to seek professional support for stuck points, complex health histories, or when they want to integrate VNS with therapy. Clinical guidance shapes your journey so you get the best fit for your body and your goals, not just a standard protocol.

When you attend a first clinical visit, you'll notice that a thorough intake sets the tone. Sharing your cardiovascular history—arrhythmias, blood pressure fluctuations, even fainting spells—helps the team screen for potential risks. Neurological issues such as seizures, migraines, or syncopal episodes are equally relevant. Don't forget about skin history if you've ever reacted to adhesives or metals—the classic concern for anyone who's had rashes under medical tape. If you have implanted devices such as pacemakers or defibrillators, mention them right away, as they may interact with certain forms of VNS (Henrique et al., 2023). Listing all medications and supplements allows clinicians to anticipate how VNS might blend or clash; for example, sedatives or sleep aids could deepen relaxation effects while stimulants might counteract them or hide subtle shifts. You remain the expert on your lived experience, so voice clear, measurable aims for your care: "lower panic attacks from five a week to two," "fall asleep within 20 minutes," or "avoid needing to leave work meetings early." Defining outcomes helps set expectations for both you and your provider, turning disclosure into a tool rather than a hurdle.

Clinical teams bring a responsive approach to session design. Instead of static routines, you'll see careful tweaks based on how your mind and body react. They adjust session length, intensity, on/off-duty cycles, and weekly schedules—all guided by your logs and feedback. Say you notice agitation after morning sessions; a clinician might move your practice to the evenings, when your nervous system tends toward rest and recovery. Or, if you hit a plateau in progress, they could suggest adding a brief session before an anticipated stressor, such as a public speaking event or commute. This kind of personalization isn't trial-and-error; it's grounded in patient reports and symptom tracking, which research shows are cornerstones of successful VNS care (Henrique et al., 2023). Stable improvement also opens the door to gradual scaling: for example, layering in an extra five-minute session before situations that trigger anxiety, as long as you continue feeling steady and supported.

Pairing VNS with talk therapy or body-based approaches multiplies the benefits. When bottom-up methods like VNS combine with top-down strategies—including cognitive behavioural therapy (CBT) for patterns of thinking, acceptance and commitment therapy (ACT) for values-guided action, or somatic work for body awareness—you build stronger gains. A five-minute VNS session before exposure work can lower arousal enough that facing distressing memories doesn't overwhelm you, making cognitive restructuring more accessible (Powers et al., 2025). Remember the orienting practices from Chapter 6, like scanning the body for tension, and the breathwork from Chapter 4, to nudge your nervous system toward calm. Coordinating the timing of therapy homework and VNS gives each skill a boost; practicing grounding techniques at home the day after your therapy appointment, paired with a short VNS session, can solidify new habits. Planning with your provider so VNS amplifies—but never replaces—therapy, keeps you in the driver's seat and draws on evidence for combining brain and body interventions (Henrique et al., 2023; Powers et al., 2025).

Tracking meaningful change is easier with objective markers. Rather than only rating your mood, use weekly logs with columns like Sleep Quality (0-10), number and duration of panic episodes, and function wins—such as finishing a work task, staying for a whole family meal, or driving without stopping. Report how long it takes you to fall asleep (sleep onset latency), how many times you wake up, and how refreshed you feel on waking. Documenting triggers alongside panic counts highlights connections, helping both you and your clinician spot trends that feelings alone might hide. Functional improvements—like attending three social events in a week instead of avoiding them, or completing an exercise class—show real-life gains that matter more than daily emotional ups and downs. These metrics let your care team fine-tune protocols to keep progress visible and sustainable (Henrique et al., 2023).

Modern VNS paths—from home-based practice up to collaborative clinical care—give you tools that scale with your needs. Instead of replacing your autonomy, clinician collaboration extends it, bringing clarity and backup for hard-to-solve problems. As you look to Chapter 8's 7-Day Calm Sprint, remember that both solo and guided approaches support consistency, growth, and lasting relief.

Chapter 8

FROM THEORY TO ROUTINE: YOUR 7-DAY CALM SPRINT

When simple, consistent actions replaced overwhelming routines, Lena, a 34-year-old nurse, began to see immediate improvements. She struggled with cycles of panic and restless nights for years, and long routines left her more overwhelmed. Trying a one-week micro-practice plan, she committed to two brief daily sessions of breathwork plus somatic touch or sound, noting her calm level before and after. By day three, her scores doubled, breath rate improved, and afternoon panic was absent. Small steps bring fast results, reinforcing results.

By the seventh day, Lena discovered that pairing humming with a gentle neck glide eased her 'wired and tired' feelings better than breath alone. These two practices became staples in her daily routine. Inspired by her progress, this chapter will walk you through the exact sprint design she followed. It offers a clear, manageable structure you can use to develop your own calming routine, focusing on brief, targeted sessions paired with mindful tracking. Starting small and building routine connections can quickly help you find what works best for your nervous system, just as Lena did.

Sprint Design and Rules

This 7-day Calm Sprint anchors your calming tools in a real, manageable routine you can start now. You've gathered science-backed techniques, and now you'll use a supportive structure that balances autonomy and safety. Don't worry about starting from zero—build from what you already have.

A daily rhythm of two short sessions is central—just five to seven minutes each, morning and evening. This brief, regular pattern entrains your nervous system: practicing at these times teaches your mind and body to anticipate calm. Setting your physiological baseline with a morning session before the stress of the day, and winding down at night, guides smoother transitions and reduces anxiety's hold. As little as six minutes in the morning primes you for resilience, and evening practice preps you for restful sleep.

You might worry about choosing and doing everything perfectly—perfection isn't the point. Instead of following a strict script, you'll be choosing from a Daily Protocol Menu, which means you get autonomy within boundaries. In each session, pick one breath practice and pair it with either somatic touch or a sound-based technique. This pairing draws on multiple pathways to activate your vagus nerve—breath shifts heart rhythms, while touch and sound bring in interoceptive signaling and acoustic stimulation. The effect is stronger when you use more than one pathway at once. Don't stress about consistency across the week; permission to adjust is part of the plan. If resonant breathing plus hand-on-heart soothes you on Monday but leaves you jittery on Wednesday, try switching to humming plus orienting. Your nervous system may need different input day to day, and honoring those shifts is not only allowed, but it's also smart.

Choice carries another benefit—research shows that autonomy supports regulation, making it easier to stick with changes and avoid decision fatigue. Having a clear, yet flexible, menu keeps things simple. With only two elements to combine, you never spend precious willpower debating fifteen possibilities. Trust that your selections are enough; picking from the menu preserves your energy for practice rather than draining it on unnecessary decisions.

Tracking your progress brings meaning and motivation to your work. That's why each practice starts and ends with a quick check-in using a 0–10 calm score. This echoes the measurement strategies you learned earlier in Chapter 2. Before you begin, standing in your kitchen or sitting in your favorite chair, pause and rate how calm you feel right now. Immediately after finishing, still in that same spot, rate again. Numbers matter, but so do brief written notes: jotting "jaw softer," "shoulders dropped," or "still feeling buzzy" captures what your body is telling you, even if numbers shift a little. Over time, these scores and notes reveal patterns—for example, your midday ratings may rise faster than your evening scores, indicating which time of day supports change better. This guides you in refining your practice, turning small experiments into powerful feedback loops for your unique system.

Rest and titration are built in for balance and effectiveness. The midpoint, day four, is a planned reset: switch to gentler practices and shorten sessions if you feel depleted. Like strength training, your nervous system benefits from these lighter intervals. This balance prepares you to handle high-intensity moments and tailors your routine for long-term success.

Every element here serves your success: predictable structure lowers anxiety and increases follow-through, while built-in choice and self-kindness let you adapt without guilt. Soon, you'll see exactly what practices belong in your "menu" for each part of the day, and learn how to blend breath, touch, and sound for maximum vagal engagement. For now, trust that committing to small, regular efforts that feel safe and manageable is exactly the path your body needs.

Daily Protocol Menu

With the structure of your 7-day sprint in place, you're ready to put technique into action. Lena's story from the beginning of this chapter showed that even simple pairings, like breathing with touch or sound, can help dial back anxiety quickly—often by Day 3, her calm score had moved up by 2 full points using these menus. This menu gives you options for morning, midday, and evening sessions, each crafted so you can choose what feels right and track real changes with each practice (Galdino, 2025).

Morning Options: Two-Step Pairings for Calm Starts

Pick either protocol below as your morning anchor. Try both during your first few days, then stick with the one that helps your calm score rise by at least one point in under ten minutes.

Option 1: Resonant Breathing + Orienting

- Sit upright in a chair, feet flat or cross-legged on the floor.
- Inhale through your nose for 5-6 seconds, then exhale gently through your mouth for 5-6 seconds. Repeat this cycle 10 times.
- Let your breath be easy and unforced; your belly should move softly. Settle into the rhythm until it feels smooth.
- Now, add orienting: Slowly name five things you see around you—colors, shapes, movement. Next, list up to five sounds or sensations (like the hum of a fridge or warmth on skin). Spend 30-60 seconds just noticing these cues for safety and familiarity.
- If at any time you feel rushed or distracted, pause the breath count and focus on naming cues instead. Notice if your chest and shoulders relax as your mind settles (Galdino, 2025).

Option 2: Humming + Neck Glide

- Begin seated. Take a comfortable inhale, then hum as you exhale for 6-8 seconds. Your lips should buzz, and you'll feel the vibration in your chest and face.
- Keep your voice relaxed—not too loud or forced. Repeat for six to eight breaths.

- After humming, turn your head slowly side-to-side, moving your chin toward each shoulder. Move gently, without pushing past resistance. Aim for 5-6 slow passes per side.
- Choose this pairing if you prefer gentle movement and sound, or if it helps your body soften more than breath alone. Track your pre- and post-session calm rating to guide your choice (MEMT Dissertation and Thesis Catalog, 2025).

No matter which routine you pick, the goal is to practice something that feels doable every day. Personal preference matters most here—honor what feels easier to maintain, not what seems "best" on paper. If neither option lifts your calm by at least one level, experiment—combine pieces or shorten steps as needed (Galdino, 2025).

Midday Reset: Fast Relief for Busy Moments

This protocol prevents tension from building unchecked when stress spikes in the middle of your workday, during the school run, or while making dinner.

- Sitting or standing, inhale deeply through the nose. Take a second small sip of air on top of the first big inhale—almost like a double sniff. Then, open your mouth and exhale fully and slowly. This is called a physiological sigh, and it works by quickly reducing nervous system arousal.
- Repeat for about 60 seconds—usually four to five cycles.

- Add your non-dominant hand over the center of your chest, covering your sternum. Let your palm rest gently, or use soft, back-and-forth strokes.
- Try this right after a difficult email, before stepping into a tense meeting, or anytime shoulders creep up toward your ears. You'll likely notice chest tightness easing and thoughts growing quieter inside a minute (Galdino, 2025; MEMT Dissertation and Thesis Catalog, 2025).

Evening Wind-Down: Signal Off-Duty Mode

You need a routine that signals your nervous system to let go, especially when home responsibilities or late-night worries linger. A short body scan pairs well with gentle rocking, prepping you for rest no matter your living space or sleep challenges.

- Lie down or sit comfortably. Starting at your feet, bring attention to each part of your body—calves, knees, thighs, hips, stomach, chest, arms, hands, neck, face, scalp. Spend only 5-10 seconds on each spot. Just notice sensation, temperature, or pressure—no need to change anything.
- After scanning, gently rock your knees or torso side to side, no more than 1-2 centimetres of movement. Stay with this subtle rhythm for one to two minutes.
- If thoughts rush in, let exhales stretch out (four counts in, six to seven counts out) while you keep rocking. There's no performance to get right—just let the motion soothe you into winding down (Galdino, 2025).

Swap Rule: Safety First, Always

If any practice brings on discomfort—like breath hunger, dizziness, rising heat, irritability, or an urge to stop—shift instantly into your lightest option. These include naming safe objects or sounds around you (orienting), placing your hand comfortingly on your heart, or humming lightly for 30-60 seconds. Choosing gentleness protects your gains and prevents setbacks. Each swap is smart self-regulation, not a sign of weakness. When you do swap, jot a quick note: date, which practice you started, what you felt, which safer option you shifted to, and how your calm score changed afterward. This running log will help shape your long-term plan by week's end.

There's permission to mix, match, and adapt these routines without guilt, as every session teaches you more about your own nervous system. Use your 0-10 calm scores to steer your choices, aiming for practices that reliably move you up one point or more each time. The foundation built here sets you up to add lifestyle tweaks in the coming days—think of this as your warm-up for deeper, lasting calm (Galdino, 2025; MEMT Dissertation and Thesis Catalog, 2025).

Food, Sleep, and Light Tweaks

Building on your morning and evening practice sessions, the last two days have probably shown you how much daily rhythm matters. When meals are skipped or sleep runs short, breathwork or body scans can feel more difficult. While your breathwork creates immediate calm, it rests on a foundation of food, rest, light, and hydration. These behind-the-scenes players quietly shape the body's stress response—and with a few tweaks, they multiply the calming power of every technique you've learned.

Stable meals act like anchors for your nervous system. When meals are irregular or made up entirely of quick carbs, blood sugar swings can make the body feel anxious: shakiness, irritability, and even a racing heart all follow drops in glucose, thanks to cortisol surges that try to rescue you (Smith & Jones, 2020). Because these sensations mimic anxiety, it's easy to assume practices aren't working when, in reality, your body is simply running low on fuel. Eating every 3-4 hours helps maintain steady energy levels. Pairing protein, complex carbohydrates, and healthy fats helps slow digestion and keeps glucose more stable. Try overnight oats with walnuts and berries at breakfast, a roasted chicken wrap with hummus for lunch, or Greek yogurt with seeds and apple as an afternoon snack. No meal plan survives every day unchanged—sometimes late meetings or kids' schedules get in the way. That's where a slow-carb snack, like peanut butter on whole-grain toast or a handful of roasted chickpeas, smooths over the gap without a big insulin spike. Observing how different foods affect your sense of calm, using a simple tracking grid, helps clarify if certain choices amplify your practice results.

Caffeine offers both ritual comfort and focus, but its hidden effects can linger far longer than the morning buzz suggests. The average half-life of caffeine is around 6 hours, which means that 8-10 hours after a cup, about one-quarter of it is still circulating and blocking adenosine receptors—the brain's signal for sleep pressure (Brown et al., 2019). This blockage can push your body's alertness into the evening, making restful sleep harder to access and dampening overnight recovery. If you've noticed trouble falling asleep or feeling jittery during afternoon practice, setting an 'afternoon curfew'—for example, switching to decaf after 2 pm—helps test how caffeine affects you personally. Sensitivity is highly individual; some need to stop earlier, while others tolerate more. For anyone not ready to cut back fully, pairing coffee with eggs or nuts blunts the spike in cortisol and insulin that sharpens anxiety. Changing beverage routines isn't easy—see this phase as an experiment, a chance to discover whether shifting timing or dose changes your sleep or calm score over just a week.

Sleep forms the bedrock for everything in this sprint. Remember from Chapter 2 that HRV fluctuates with quality of rest; deep, consistent sleep helps vagal tone rebound overnight and improves the next day's practice outcomes (Miller & Lane, 2018). Small changes add up: winding down with dim lighting, keeping screens on warm-tone filters after sunset, and reducing noise in the bedroom each prompt melatonin release. Aim to keep a similar sleep window, even if bedtime needs to adapt to life demands. People often believe a poor night can be fixed with just more willpower, but the nervous system needs real rest to recalibrate its baseline.

Light hygiene fine-tunes the body's internal clock, led by the suprachiasmatic nucleus—a cluster in the brain that syncs your schedule to the environment. Morning light exposure signals the brain to suppress melatonin and triggers the first cortisol surge for energy (Walker et al., 2019). Even on cloudy days, the light outside is dozens of times stronger than artificial lamps. Stepping onto a balcony, opening curtains, or sitting near a window for ten minutes as soon as possible after waking establishes a healthy rhythm. Evening routines flip the signal: lights dim and screens switch to night mode, easing the transition to parasympathetic dominance. If outdoor time isn't safe or feasible, standing at a bright window still provides benefit. This circadian alignment underpins the improvements in HRV and emotional stability discussed earlier (Walker et al., 2019).

Hydration habits support every system related to calm. When you're dehydrated, blood volume drops slightly, which can trigger sympathetic arousal as the body tries to keep blood pressure up—often leading to feelings of dizziness or unease that mirror anxiety (Johnson & Stein, 2017). Checking urine color—pale yellow points to good hydration—offers a quick feedback loop. People who notice lightheadedness when standing may do better with electrolytes (like a pinch of salt or a sugar-free electrolyte powder) added to water, not just fluid volume. Pairing a moment of slow breathing with each refill turns hydration into a cue for a mini reset and gradually builds habit strength. This prevents dehydration from sneaking up on you on busy days and connects body care directly to your nervous system's signals.

Adjusting several habits at once can feel like juggling too many balls. It's normal to find one tweak easier than another. Change works best as a series of experiments—if spacing meals feels overwhelming, focus on light exposure for a few days, then revisit food rhythm later. Tracking your practice quality alongside these variables lays the groundwork for the reflection stage coming next. Soon, you'll spot amplifiers—personal tweaks that double the benefits of your chosen techniques. When supportive routines and active practices join forces, they create a solid platform for calm that lasts well beyond this sprint.

Sprint Reflection and Adjustment

You've just lived seven days observing, tracking, and experimenting with new calm-building practices—backed by stable meals, regular hydration, and steady light habits that made everything easier to notice and record. Your journal or app is full of numbers and quick notes from each session. This raw information is your launchpad. By pausing now to reflect, you transform scattered data into useful routines you can actually stick with. Take out your journal, grab a pen, and move through these prompts to turn experiments into next steps tailored for you.

Best 2 Practices: Which Felt Easiest and Most Effective?

Start by reviewing the entire week's calm scores and any quick impressions or body sensations you wrote down. Scan for two techniques that brought reliable boosts—a one or two-point rise in calm score happened almost every time, and these sessions never felt forced or draining. Usually, ease and effectiveness go hand in hand: a practice that fits your body's needs is repeated, which helps retrain your nervous system faster (Team, 2024). Circle both. Next, write down one sentence for each circled practice: What worked? Was it humming that softened jaw tension by day three? Did neck glide clear the "wired and tired" feeling before bed better than breathing alone, like Lena found? Describe what changed inside you. Now, look at those two practices and choose one to become your anchor ritual for the next week—the non-negotiable habit you slip into every day, no matter what comes up. Anchoring gives your routine a dependable center as you keep exploring what works best for you (How to Approach Sprints in Agile Project Management: 3 Recommendations, 2024).

Red Flags: What Signs Showed You Needed Less Intensity?

Every experiment provides feedback, not only on what worked but also on where you hit limits. Glance over your notes and look for any time anxiety spiked instead of settled, or when your body said "enough." Maybe breath holds left you dizzy, cold exposure made you nauseous, or orienting led to restlessness. These red flags are not setbacks—they're guideposts showing where your window of tolerance is for now (Team, 2024). Write a short list using clear body language: "Felt chest tightness after humming," or "Numb feet after kneeling." Then, for each one, pair it with a gentle alternative: "If physiological sighs made me restless, I could switch to slow nasal breathing with hand on belly." Set up one concrete If-Then plan: "If I feel buzzed or numb midway, I will pause and orient with a soft touch for 30 seconds." This protects hard-won comfort, honors your nervous system's signals, and builds self-trust for future rounds (How to Approach Sprints in Agile Project Management: 3 Recommendations, 2024).

Timing Fit: When in the Day Worked Best?

Go back through your tracker and compare calm scores after morning and evening sessions. Notice which time consistently moved your baseline up, which was easiest to do without distractions, and which felt almost automatic—like brushing your teeth. Ask yourself: "Did morning humming make the work day less jagged? Did the evening neck glide reset my mood after a long afternoon? Which slot turned into a break I looked forward to rather than something I had to force?" Use these clues to adjust your schedule. If mornings give the biggest gains and fit smoothly, plan your anchor practice there. If afternoons are filled with interruptions or evenings become stressful, shift accordingly (Team, 2024). Consistency at the chosen time wires your brain to expect and respond to your cues faster, making progress smoother with less effort (How to Approach Sprints in Agile Project Management: 3 Recommendations, 2024).

Next Week Plan: Keep One, Modify One, Add One New Micro-Practice

Here's how you shape your evolving routine so it stays fresh and doable. First, write down the exact anchor practice you chose to "keep"—no changes, just commit to it daily. Second, pick one other technique that helped but didn't quite fit, and decide how you'll tweak it based on what you learned. Maybe you shorten the session, lower the intensity, or swap the context (try a neck glide in the morning instead of at night). Third, choose a single new micro-practice to add—a sixty-second trial run of something new, a mix-and-match variation, or a tool you skipped. Write each step as a commitment in your journal: "I will keep [X] every day, modify [Y], and add [Z] as an experiment to track." This "keep-modify-add" approach strikes the right balance between stability and exploration, supporting steady growth at your own pace (Team, 2024).

Your week of reflection closes the loop on this first sprint and arms you with the personal instructions you need for tougher days ahead. This is your bridge to handling high-pressure moments and, soon, building a truly personal calm toolkit that keeps pace as your capacity grows (How to Approach Sprints in Agile Project Management: 3 Recommendations, 2024).

Chapter 9

HANDLING HIGH-INTENSITY MOMENTS

This toolkit offers small, practical protocols you can use any time anxiety strikes. These strategies start with quick physical resets to calm your body and prevent anxious spirals. No special space or long session is needed—each move is made for real-life moments, like waiting in line, riding a crowded train, or pausing at your desk.

In this chapter, you'll learn a four-step panic sequence you can use immediately, wherever you are. The steps move your focus through senses, breath, touch, and gentle movement, creating crucial space between fear and action and signaling safety to your nervous system. Practicing this real-time sequence gives you accessible tools to regain calm and clarity quickly during high-intensity moments.

Panic Protocol in Your Pocket

Panic is your body's alarm system, not a failure. When your heart pounds or your chest tightens in public or at work, anxiety can feel unbreakable. This protocol is designed for those exact moments: small, clear actions you can use anywhere, like standing in line or sitting on a crowded train. By targeting your body first, each step calms physical panic before your mind spirals.

Step 1: Ground: Name Your Senses and Anchor Yourself

Step 1 uses your senses to ground you in the present and interrupts panic fast. Sensory input signals the thinking brain (prefrontal cortex) to quiet the body's emergency response (amygdala) (Center for Substance Abuse Treatment (US), 2014).

Start by observing five things you can see. Say them quietly out loud, or whisper them in your head if you're not comfortable speaking. For example, "I see the blue chair, the silver doorframe, a red scarf, my shoes, the poster with green letters." Next, notice four things you can touch—maybe your sleeve, the cool metal of a seat edge, the firm grip of your phone, or the warm fabric of your pants. Then bring attention to three sounds, even quiet ones, like the hum of lights, distant voices, or the rumble in your own stomach. Gently search for two smells; this could be pencil wood, fabric softener, or maybe you need to shift slightly to find a scent. Finally, check for one thing you can taste—gum, coffee, or simply the air in your mouth (Smith, 2018).

Naming each sense out loud matters because language centers compete with panic circuits, giving your calmer brain a foothold. Finish this step by pressing your feet down. Notice where your weight settles, the pressure through your soles, the texture or temperature beneath you. If standing isn't possible, press your hands into your thighs or grip your chair's arms. Even twenty seconds spent grounding creates needed space between fear and action (Center for Substance Abuse Treatment (US), 2014).

Step 2: Breath: Change the Chemistry Quickly

Breathing acts as an emergency brake for panic. When anxiety is high, CO2 builds up in the blood, making you feel more short of breath, dizzy, or trapped. Both breathing options offered here reset this system. You can choose either based on what feels accessible in the moment.

Option A: Physiological sigh. Inhale gently through your nose to fill most of your lungs. Pause, then take a small extra sip to expand your chest. Now exhale slowly through your mouth, emptying your lungs and letting your shoulders drop. Repeat two or three rounds. This method rapidly reduces tension and lowers CO2 levels.

Option B: 1:2 Breath. Inhale through your nose for a slow count of four. Let your jaw hang loose as you exhale for a count of eight. Focus on the sensation of your shoulders dropping and your belly relaxing. One or two rounds are enough to start lowering the alarm in your body (Center for Substance Abuse Treatment (US), 2014).

The main idea is: Short bursts of breathing are the goal—not perfection. If taking a breath feels overwhelming, skip ahead and return to this step later. Your breath doesn't have to be silent or smooth; it just needs to be present.

Step 3 Touch: Send Safety Signals Through Contact

Touch is a direct way to interrupt panic by sending your body safety signals. Place one hand over your heart, sense warmth through clothes, feel the gentle weight, and track your breath under your palm.

For added effect, cross your arms over your chest and tap each hand on the opposite arm, left then right, at about one tap per second. This motion, called bilateral stimulation, helps integrate the jolt of panic across both sides of your brain, processing arousal so it doesn't stay stuck. Use gentle—not forceful—pressure. Some people like pairing touch with a soft phrase, like "I'm here," but this is always optional. Self-touch works whether you're alone or in public. If self-touch draws unwanted attention, try pressing thumb to forefinger under a desk or in a pocket instead (Center for Substance Abuse Treatment (US), 2014).

Step 4 Orient: Prove to Your Brain That You Are Safe

To show your brain you are safe and have choices, turn your head slowly side to side, resting your eyes on neutral or pleasant details—a person reading, an exit sign, a smile, or your bag. This cues your nervous system that danger is not immediate and restores a sense of control. Noticing exits is about building agency, not escape.

After two or three sweeps, rate your distress on a scale from 0 to 10. If you're still above a 7, return to Step 1 and repeat. If lower, experiment with daily activities or add a longer grounding practice (Smith, 2018).

Imagine Maya on the train: her chest tight, palms clammy, but she starts quietly naming what she sees and feels. She grounds her feet, breathes once, and presses her hand to her heart. A slow turn of her head spots a familiar magazine cover. Her panic shifts—not cured, but softened.

If you can't speak aloud, name things in your mind. If your feet don't touch the floor, anchor with your hands. When breath is scary, start somewhere else. This sequence is a guide, not a test. If pain, true breath restriction, or severe dizziness appear, get medical help—it's always appropriate to check. Practicing in calm moments makes these steps easier when they matter most. Even getting through the first two steps often changes the trajectory of panic. Know that every try counts, and recovery from panic does not demand perfection.

Interrupting Mental Spirals: Four Everyday Off-Ramps to Calm the Mind

Breaking out of the cycle of lingering, post-panic racing thoughts is crucial for anyone seeking steady energy for work, relationships, or a sense of ease. Many people, even after the physical signs of panic fade, find their minds still spinning—echoes that keep the body on alert even when danger has passed (Curtiss et al., 2021; Beck et al., 2005). The following tools are designed to guide you from worry back to clarity in everyday moments, whether you're in line, at your desk, or commuting. You just need a willingness to experiment and observe what helps your mind return to a neutral state. These mental off-ramps build on physical grounding techniques, connecting thought and body for lasting calm (Hofmann et al., 2020).

Labelling: Naming the Thought Loop

Picture yourself replaying a tense meeting, caught in "what if" questions and stuck in worst-case scenarios. Labelling is about noticing these sticky thoughts, then gently naming them ("worry," "planning," "judging") to create some distance.

How to do it:

1. Pause and take a slow breath.
2. Hear or see the thought that's repeating. Instead of wrestling with it, mentally say or whisper a simple label. Options include:

   "This is a worry."

   "Here's planning."

   "That's fear showing up again."
3. Picture the thought as an object—a cloud, a car, or a leaf—drifting by. Watch it move, knowing it can pass without pulling you along.
4. If labelling makes you self-conscious, try quietly writing the word on your phone or notebook.
5. Notice any shift, like a slight drop in tension or a longer exhale.

Some people feel silly or awkward at first. That's normal. If your mind argues, acknowledge the push-back ("Doubt is here too") and keep going. This step is about opening space, not fixing every thought. With practice, naming will begin to loosen the grip of rumination (Hofmann & Otto, 2017).

Exhale Anchor: Steadying with Breath

After a surge of anxiety, restless thoughts can keep shoulders tense or breath shallow. The exhale anchor gives mind and body one job—to follow a gentle out-breath, letting the nervous system unwind (Bandealy et al., 2021).

Steps to try:

1. Sit or stand upright, feet steady on the ground. Let your hands rest comfortably.
2. Inhale naturally. As you breathe out, pay close attention to the full path of the exhale—notice its softness, the way your chest lowers, or the sound it makes.
3. To anchor focus, count silently ("one"), trace your thumb with a finger, or press your feet down as you exhale.
4. Repeat for three to five breaths. After each round, check your body: Are your shoulders lower? Is your jaw less tight?
5. If breath work feels too intense, just place your hand over your belly to feel warmth and steadiness instead.

This approach works well in public spaces, offering a quiet reset. Some may prefer to combine the anchor with a small movement, like tapping a finger or swaying slightly in a chair. If dizziness or discomfort grows, let yourself pause and return to a simple observation—feeling gravity, sensing contact with your seat. The goal is gentle re-centring, not perfection (Beck et al., 2005).

Compassion Cue: Re-Engaging Kindness

When anxious loops revolve around mistakes or social slip-ups, self-criticism often takes center stage. A compassion cue steps in here. Instead of arguing with negative thoughts, offer yourself the kind response you'd give a friend.

To practice:

1. Notice a harsh thought ("I messed up again").
2. Gently touch two fingers to your wrist or collarbone as a signal—like turning on a light.
3. Silently repeat a phrase such as:

   "It's okay to feel this way."

   "Others struggle too."

   "I'm allowed to learn."
4. Try this inside your head while walking, waiting for the bus, or washing dishes.
5. Watch for changes—a sigh, a hint of softening in your face, or a moment of relief.

For those who feel clumsy with self-kindness, start with "This is tough, and I'm here." Skip any phrase that feels forced. Even a single compassionate gesture can open enough space for anxiety to loosen (Bandealy et al., 2021).

Movement Pulse: Discharge and Reset

Sometimes thinking keeps looping because the body still holds onto an extra charge. Simple movement pulses release pent-up energy, freeing both body and mind.

You might try:

- Standing and shifting weight side to side, focusing on how your feet feel against the ground.
- Rolling your shoulders forward and back while breathing out.

- Gently rocking in a chair or bouncing heels beneath your desk.

Keep movements small if you're in public. If you're at home, stretching arms overhead or swaying to music can help clear the last traces of worry. Check in afterward: Is your breath deeper? Do your hands feel warmer? If movement increases agitation, let yourself return to stillness or another favorite technique (Bandealy et al., 2021).

Progress Checks and Safety Boundaries

Letting go of rumination is not about forcing thoughts away but giving your mind a new track. Each time you use a tool, watch for subtle signals—calmer breath, relaxed muscles, and a sense of greater presence. If distress rises, remind yourself it's safe to skip or change steps. Worry returning is part of learning. Every attempt counts, and the toolkit grows with practice. Keep layering these mental resets alongside your body-based skills. Over time, linking these exercises together helps create a steadier baseline and plants seeds for resilience (Curtiss et al., 2021; Bandealy et al., 2021).

Overwhelm to Neutral in Three Minutes

When intense stress hits at work, on public transport, or anywhere you feel trapped by your own physiology, it's easy to freeze or spiral into panic. This section builds directly on your growing body-awareness from previous chapters and gives you accessible, subtle resets you can use right where you are—no special tools or privacy required. These brief protocols aren't about willpower but about quickly signaling safety to your nervous system, so you can regain composure, think clearly, and carry on with your day. Each mini-exercise is designed for health-conscious adults who want fast, reliable ways to shift anxious states without drawing attention.

Micro-Exhale Sets: Rapid Downshift Breathing

Target areas: Respiratory system, vagus nerve activation, shoulder, and jaw relaxation

Difficulty: Beginner

Duration: About 1 minute

Steps:

1. Sit or stand comfortably, keeping your spine upright and your shoulders relaxed, away from your ears.
2. Inhale quietly through your nose for 2 seconds, keeping jaw and throat soft.
3. Exhale gently for 4 seconds through the nose or pursed lips; feel your belly soften, not bracing.
4. Repeat this inhale-exhale cycle for 6 sets, using your fingers to discreetly count in your pocket or under a desk.
5. If you notice dizziness or breath hunger, switch to normal breathing for 30 seconds before starting again, then resume when ready.

This technique is supported by evidence showing exhale-focused breathing produces acute mood improvements and rapid physiological downshifts (Balban et al., 2023). It's also recommended as a staple calming tool in major self-care guides (NHS, 2021).Palm Cool: Reset via Temperature Target areas: Palms, forearms, sensory pathways to the brain

Difficulty: Beginner

Duration: 30–60 seconds per hand

Steps:

1. Grab a cool can, water bottle, or any chilled object available nearby.
2. Wrap your palm fully around the cool surface and hold for 15–30 seconds.
3. Switch hands partway through to avoid numbness or discomfort, especially if sensitivity is high.
4. As you hold the item, pair each slow exhale with the cooling sensation (aim for one complete exhale every 5 seconds).
5. If no cold item is available, run your wrists briefly under cool water for 20–30 seconds, switching between sides.

This physical reset capitalizes on your body's innate 'cooling reflex,' lowering perceived stress and helping focus return. It is gentle enough for nearly any setting and requires only what you may have on hand.

Soft Gaze: Peripheral Vision Reset

Target areas: Eyes, facial muscles, visual cortex, neck, and upper back

Difficulty: Beginner

Duration: 10–20 seconds

Steps:

1. Sit or stand quietly, without moving your head.
2. Let your eyes become aware of the far left and right edges of your field of vision—the room's corners, window frames, or outer objects.
3. Allow your gaze to soften slightly, as if you're looking past your screen or through it, not at one point.
4. Smooth your forehead and relax the skin around your eyes; add a gentle half-smile to reduce jaw tension.
5. Maintain this soft, wide gaze for 10–20 seconds while continuing natural breaths.

This technique helps open awareness and signals the nervous system that there is no immediate threat, aiding the transition away from the tunnel vision that accompanies stress. Use it whenever you notice your attention narrowing or feel hyper-focused on perceived danger.

Neck Wrap: Containment Touch

Target areas: Sides of neck, collarbones, upper chest (skin and fascia), limbic safety networks

Difficulty: Beginner

Duration: 30–60 seconds

Steps:

1. Take a light scarf, hoodie, or adjust your shirt collar so it lightly contacts the sides of your neck and/or top of your chest.

2. Ensure pressure is gentle, more like a soft containment than squeezing; avoid covering or pressing on the throat itself.
3. Breathe slowly, noticing the warmth and gentle contact. Imagine sensation spreading comfort across your upper chest.
4. Stay here for 30–60 seconds, using slow nasal breaths with extended exhales if possible.
5. If touch near the neck is unpleasant or feels unsafe, try holding a weighted lap item (like a bag) or crossing your arms for a self-hug instead.

This exercise taps into the body's need for gentle boundary cues during arousal, offering somatic reassurance and a fast sense of being 'collected.' It prepares you for re-engaging with tasks after disruption.

These protocols are intentionally crafted to fit urban and workplace life—quick, unnoticeable, and effective in restoring a neutral state. Each one is anchored in signals your nervous system understands: breath rhythm, temperature, visual input, and safe touch. Use them separately or stack two together if time allows. Remember, safety and progress sometimes mean reaching out for outside support when intensity remains high. In the next section, you'll learn how to recognize those moments when professional care or crisis planning is most appropriate, including which symptoms and plateaus to watch for.

When to Seek More Support

The pocket protocols you've practiced in this chapter offer fast, reliable relief for many anxiety spikes—but recognizing when to seek additional support is just as essential to your safety and progress. While quick resets can steady you through most surges of panic, rumination, or overwhelm, some moments call for a different kind of help. Full recovery involves knowing both what you can do right now and when reaching outside yourself is the strongest move you can make.

Red Flags That Require Immediate Care

Act quickly if you notice sudden or intense changes in your body or awareness. Chest pain, shortness of breath, fainting, or severe dizziness are not typical signs of anxiety alone—these need urgent evaluation by medical professionals to rule out heart problems and other critical causes (Center, 2025). If you lose track of time, feel disconnected from reality for long stretches, or suddenly cannot remember where you are or how you got there, these dissociative symptoms signal it's time to reach out for professional mental health care (Center, 2025; Spa, 2023).

Look for emotional warning signs like extreme irritability, severe mood swings, or explosive outbursts that don't match your usual self. Pulling away from people, neglecting daily responsibilities, or saying things like "I'm a burden" can also point to an underlying crisis—even if you think the cause is clear (Center, 2025). Don't downplay expressions of worthlessness or thoughts about death and suicide. These are not just part of having a tough day; fast action and direct support are needed (Spa, 2023). For physical changes, pay attention to new sleep problems, significant weight or appetite changes, neglecting hygiene, or unexplained pain. Any combination of these symptoms, especially if they appear together or escalate quickly, means a check-in with your doctor or therapist is the next best step (Center, 2025).

Navigating Stuck Patterns With Self-Awareness

Beyond immediate resets, some patterns show up more quietly over time. If you've used the practices in this book daily for four to six weeks and notice your anxiety ratings staying high or recovery times growing longer—not shorter—that's valuable feedback. Use a simple system: track your peak anxiety each week and measure how quickly you return to calm after each spike. When those numbers stall or worsen rather than improve, consider this evidence that deeper support could unlock the next phase of growth (Center, 2025).

Seeking therapy, coaching, or group programs does not mean your efforts have failed—it shows you're listening to your body and mind. Outside input may help reveal invisible obstacles, such as trauma or unspoken stressors, that techniques alone can't fully address (Spa, 2023). You might choose to reassess your routines or ask a provider for an extra layer of guidance. Plateaus happen for almost everyone; the right question is not, "Why am I stuck?" but "Who can help me get unstuck?"

Coordinating Self-Regulation With Medications

To ensure your safety as you build your practice, share every new breathwork, cold exposure, or supplement routine with your prescriber or pharmacist. Some activities can affect heart rate, blood pressure, or interact with medications already on board for anxiety, depression, or other health conditions (Center, 2025). Never adjust, skip, or double any dose without your provider's input, even if you're feeling better. Sometimes, medication side effects like jitteriness or palpitations mimic anxiety spikes and can create confusion about where sensations are coming from.

Bring your notes to appointments. Try phrases like, "I'm starting daily breathing exercises and cold showers. Are there any interactions or precautions I should know about with my current medications?" This opens the door for collaborative troubleshooting and helps reassure you that your whole care team is working alongside you. If any new symptom appears—especially if it's fast, unusual, or distressing—let your prescriber know before making any changes to your regimen (Center, 2025).

Creating and Using a Crisis Plan

Building a simple crisis plan gives you reassurance and direction during your toughest moments. Start by listing your personal early warning signs—such as sudden withdrawal, racing thoughts, worsening sleep, or talk of hopelessness (Center, 2025; Spa, 2023). Add three to five grounding steps that work for you (like a favorite pocket protocol from earlier in this chapter) and keep emergency contacts, including at least one trusted person and local crisis numbers (the 988 Suicide & Crisis Lifeline or local services), all on a one-page card.

Store copies in your wallet, on your phone, and share them with someone you trust. Once a week, read your plan out loud so the steps feel familiar, not overwhelming, if you need to do so urgently. Having a plan isn't expecting failure, but preparing for anything—just like learning CPR doesn't mean you expect a heart attack. It's a solid act of self-care and advocacy for your well-being (Center, 2025).

Taking these actions reflects the knowledge gained in Chapters 1 through 8 and the strong foundation already built. Seeking skilled help means you're supporting your own progress, not giving up control. Knowing when to call in extra support will strengthen the personalized, sustainable plan you'll develop in Chapter 10, placing you firmly in charge of your next steps.

Chapter 10

PERSONALIZATION AND PROGRESS: MAKING IT YOURS

Picture yourself three months from now, starting your day with a calming five-minute routine—slow breathing, collarbone tapping, and a splash of cold water. This steady practice grounds you, turning tense afternoons into moments of calm, all without adding stress to your life.

This chapter guides you to design your own calm by understanding your nervous system. You'll uncover what triggers your stress, learn your most effective calming actions, and build supportive habits. By noticing your body's patterns and preferences, you'll lay the groundwork for personal resilience—making calm your new normal and letting others see your steady progress.

Your Nervous System Profile: Mapping What Matters Most

Putting yourself in the driver's seat begins with learning your own nervous system landscape—what sets off anxious ripples, what reliably soothes, and how much is just right for real-world life. Start by setting aside 10 minutes in a comfortable place. Invite curiosity, not criticism.

Grab a piece of paper or open your phone notes. Think about the past week or two, and write down three situations that spark the most anxiety. These might be public places, like riding a crowded train, work settings, such as Monday meetings, or small but persistent annoyances, like late-night news scrolling. Next to each, give it an intensity score from 0 (calm) to 10 (overwhelming). For example, "Monday meetings – 7," "News scrolling before bed – 6." There's no standard scale; your numbers help track change over time, not compare with anyone else. It's normal if even 'small' events make your list, and everyone's mix is different (Lubbe & ten Ham-Baloyi, 2017).

Now, notice your early warning signs. Before anxiety rises, your body often gives small signals: a clenched jaw, tight chest, cold hands, or flushed cheeks. Jot down these physical cues, even the small ones. For example: "shoulders hunching" or "shallow breath." These gentle check-ins help you recognize patterns (Harjpal et al., 2023). Also, listen for repeated thoughts during stress, such as "What if I mess up?" or "I won't handle this." Next to each, write a simple, supportive response that offers calm without trying to fix the feeling. For example, pair "What if I mess up?" with "I can pause and breathe." If self-criticism appears, try "Noticing, not fixing; exhale for six seconds." This step is not about forcing positivity, but about inviting options when old habits return. If anything feels too intense, take a break. Remind yourself it's always okay to pause (Lubbe & ten Ham-Baloyi, 2017).

Top 3 Soothers: Discovering Your Nervous System's Favorites

Your system responds best to what you actually enjoy. Find what works by experimenting. Start with a breath exercise: take an extra-long exhale or hum for two minutes. Rate your calm, warmth, or focus on a 1–5 scale. For example: "Humming: Calm 3, Warmth 2." Next, try touch: put a hand on your heart or lightly tap your collarbone. Write down any changes you notice—maybe your jaw feels softer, or your shoulders let go. Then choose a small movement, such as neck rolls, standing sways, or shoulder shrugs. Again, notice and record your body's response (Li et al., 2022; Shaki et al., 2022). Effectiveness means what helps you personally. You might find that humming does little, but a palm over your chest settles you quickly, or that gentle movement works best for tense afternoons. If anything is uncomfortable, do less of it. Learning your body's "yes" and "no" builds trust over time (Aranha et al., 2021).

Dose Notes: Building Habits That Stick

Lasting routines are born from being kind and realistic about time and energy. Choose a starting dose—a tiny, regular block (for example, two minutes after brushing your teeth, or one minute of breathwork before the first email). Tell yourself it's okay to stay there. If you want, bump up by one minute per week, never more unless it feels natural. Connect your habit to an anchor point in your day: after commuting, before picking up kids, or alongside morning coffee. Record a daily calm score (on your own 0–10 scale) and add a one-word sleep note ("restless," "solid," "light"). This low-pressure tracking turns fleeting progress into clear wins.

Busy schedules or neurodivergent brains may call for micro-sessions—short, flexible sessions. Honoring where you are is a victory. These experiments help reveal what truly supports you, not what looks perfect on paper (Shaki et al., 2022; Lubbe & ten Ham-Baloyi, 2017).

Update Cycle: Review, Refresh, and Grow

Each month, review your notes: check trigger scores, highlight what worked, and drop what didn't. Compare your calm and sleep notes, then set one small experiment for the next month. Any improvement counts—from a lower trigger score to steadier mornings. This review process is your blueprint for deepening routines and supports real, lasting growth.

Stacking for Resilience

Now that you've mapped your triggers and calming strategies, start building resilience by layering practices. Begin with themed weeks. Instead of trying all practices at once, focus on one type each week. For example, during a 'breath week,' use the 4:6 resonant breathing (five to eight minutes in the morning and evening) and add quick resets before challenging moments, such as work meetings or evening screen time. The goal is to repeat one practice often enough that your body learns the pattern as safe and helpful. At week's end, reflect: Which breathing exercise helped most? When did anxiety drop? Which practice left you feeling calmest or most restored? These questions help you decide what to keep in your routine.

Remember the resonant breathing from Chapter 4 and the gentle neck glides from Chapter 6? Rather than attempting both daily, try dedicating one week to breath and another to movement. This lets the nervous system anchor each skill. If sound work (like humming or listening to calming music) feels grounding, plan a 'sound week' using those techniques throughout the day. By working through single-modality weeks, learning deepens and self-doubt about 'doing it right' fades, leaving more space for confidence.

The second pillar in stacking is the rule of one: change only one variable at a time. When routines get complicated, tracking what works becomes impossible. Let's say you want to test whether cold exposure boosts your sense of calm. Keep all other practices, timing, and routines steady for the week, then simply add a short, cool shower rinse at the end of your usual routine. Track how you feel—right after and thirty minutes later—with a quick check-in: "Did I feel clearer, relaxed, or wired?" This scientific approach isn't rigid; it's a tool for freedom, showing you exactly what supports your unique system (eseospaceconsulting@gmail.com, 2025).

Plan recovery days as often as you schedule high-intensity or longer sessions. Many worry that taking a step back will erase hard-won progress, but growth comes during rest just as much as active training (Tapita, 2025). On these lighter days, shorten practice times to two or three minutes, pick the gentlest versions of techniques (like hand-on-heart breathing), or spend extra time walking with a friend or pet. Watch for early signs of overwhelm—feeling 'wired and tired,' snapping at small things, struggling to fall asleep despite exhaustion, or finding that once-calming routines now spike anxiety. When any sign appears, halve your practice volume for a day or two and fill your time with soothing, restorative activities. Adjusting like this isn't giving up; it's pro-level care, slowing down to let adaptation happen (Tapita, 2025; eseospaceconsulting@gmail.com, 2025).

As seasons change, adjust your routine accordingly. Winter may need more warmth and gentle practices, while summer benefits from cooling techniques and outdoor routines. Treat seasonal shifts as reminders to adapt—true resilience comes from flexibility, not doing the same thing year-round.Stacking practices with intention builds the kind of steady, reliable nervous system flexibility that stands up to everyday stress. Weekly themes, single-variable tweaks, regular recovery, and seasonal smartness form your safety net. This strategic stacking approach doesn't just prevent overwhelm—it creates the conditions for noticing real progress. You may find yourself calmer in tough situations, sleeping better, or choosing tools on autopilot. Each step, taken at your own pace, brings you closer to seeing change where it matters most—freedom and confidence in daily life.

Milestones That Matter

Now that you've learned to stack practices without overwhelm, it's time to recognize the real-life progress that signals your nervous system is changing. Knowing the right way to practice is only half the journey—learning to see and celebrate these changes keeps motivation steady and guides you as you adjust your routine. Shifting the focus from simply counting anxious moments to noticing true capacity gains puts the spotlight on growth rather than just symptom reduction.

Recovery is a powerful sign that your regulation skills are working. Track the interval between the first cue—maybe a racing heart or tight chest—and the moment a sense of calm begins to return. If those shifts used to take 45 minutes and now settle in 8, that's neuroplastic change right before your eyes (Yehuda, 2002; Liu & Boyatzis, 2021). This kind of recovery speed shows your stress system learns safety from experience, not just theory. After each incident, jot down a quick log with the time of day, what triggered you, where you were, and which specific intervention helped most—a long exhale, cold water, or press on the collarbone. Over a week or two, these mini-logs will reveal patterns about what reliably works for you. Each reduction in bounce-back time is proof that your system is gaining flexibility and resilience, bringing you closer to sustained relief (Liu & Boyatzis, 2021).

More choice is another milestone. This means building the space between impulse and action, like pausing before snapping back at a tense email or taking a single breath before stepping into a crowded room. Counting "one-breath pauses" is a real, tangible way to measure this new control. Each pause reflects better communication between your prefrontal cortex and vagus nerve—a stronger link that helps you choose responses over reactions (Smith & Alloy, 2009; Mauss et al., 2024). Pick a script to anchor the moment: "Pause—name the feeling—exhale for 6." Reward yourself for every pause, even if it doesn't lead to perfect behavior. Celebrating the act itself teaches your nervous system that using the pause is safe and rewarding, planting seeds for future calm under pressure (Boyatzis et al., 2021).

Capacity gains appear when you can handle busier days or tougher demands without crashing later. Think of capacity as the size of the container you have for life's challenges. Maybe you could add one more meeting or a social event without needing a full day hidden away afterward. The shift from requiring 24-48 hours of recovery to bouncing back the same evening is a major win for your window of tolerance (Kessler et al., 1995; Boscarino, 1996; Gump & Matthews, 1999). Mark the beginning and end of tough stretches with short rituals: a 60-second hum or gentle tapping before, a minute or two shaking out tension after. Notice if your energy lasts longer and evenings feel more stable, even after busy days. These small increases tell you your system is becoming more adaptable and less likely to get stuck in high-alert mode, echoing the body-first principles introduced in Chapters 1 and 2 (Mauss et al., 2024).

Joy signals matter as much as tracking setbacks. Logging moments of warmth, laughter, or kindness—such as lingering eye contact or playful conversation—indicates that your nervous system is accessing ventral vagal states of ease more often (Boyatzis et al., 2021; Liu & Boyatzis, 2021). When you spot a positive spark, pair it with a soft hand on your heart or a deep, slow breath to lock in that experience and strengthen the neural pathway for future joy (Mauss et al., 2024). Prosocial actions, such as reaching out to a friend or sharing a joke, reflect growing social intelligence and the spread of emotional safety within your network (McKee & Massimilian, 2006; Fowler & Christakis, 2008). Joy is not an extra—it's one of the most reliable markers that your baseline state is shifting toward safety, creativity, and connection.

Building on your stacking experiments, these milestones give shape to your journey through the weeks ahead. They'll serve as checkpoints throughout the structured 12-week program, helping you adjust, refine, and celebrate each new cycle of growth. Every shorter recovery, honored pause, fuller day, or earned smile is proof of change unfolding in your unique way.

Your 12-Week Calm Plan: Turning Insight Into a Daily Habit

After tracking your progress in stress recovery, choice, and capacity, it's time to move into a daily system that supports real change. Seeing milestones is rewarding, but regular practice is what makes these changes stick. The coming twelve weeks offer a path forward—stepwise, flexible, and built on listening to your own nervous system.

Weeks 1–4: Build Your Base with Breath and Touch

Start each day with five minutes of calming work. Sit somewhere comfortable, let your belly soften, and breathe through your nose for four seconds. Exhale slowly—aim for six to eight seconds. Do this for three minutes. Rest one palm over the center of your chest, using just enough pressure to notice warmth and contact. Hold here for two minutes, feeling your breath and the gentle weight of your hand. If standing or kneeling aren't right for you, settle into a chair or even rest back in bed. As you finish, take note of your calm score—a quick number from zero (panic) to ten (deep peace). Log this, along with a single line about your sleep if you like, maybe in your phone's notes app or a notebook by your bed. This helps spot patterns over time (Toussaint et al., 2021).

A short evening check-in can close the day—a simple sixty seconds spent counting breaths with hand over heart. This isn't required; no need for perfection. Some days will flow better than others. If agitation grows or relaxation drops, your body might be asking for less, not more. Try trimming your morning dose to three minutes, then add a soft thirty-second hum at midday as a reset. Treat this feedback as a strength—your system wants balance (Fincham et al., 2023; Toussaint et al., 2021).

Weeks 5–8: Gentle Stress, Movement, and Cold Layers

Start bringing new elements into your routine. For three days each week, add a slow-movement session—five minutes focused on the neck, shoulders, and spine. Slide your head gently side to side, make slow circles with your shoulders, and try a seated or standing cat-cow motion. Move for sensation, not range. Let non-movement days stay restful with only breath and touch.

To add a mild challenge, end your usual shower with cool water for 10 to 20 seconds. Target the back of your neck and shoulders. The water should feel bracing but safe—never shocking. If tension increases, switch off the cold right away; go back to your base routine if needed. Afterward, track your calm score again within five minutes. Keep up with planned recovery days after big life stressors: when caring for a sick child, finishing a tough work week, or dealing with conflict, return to breath and touch basics until your sense of calm steadies (Fincham et al., 2023).

Weeks 9–12: Sound Practices and Careful Device Testing

These weeks are for refining your skills and optional exploration. Soothing sound adds a sensory experience that gently enhances vagal tone. After breathwork, spend two to three minutes humming or making long vowel sounds—a soft "ah," "oh," or "mm"—noticing vibration in lips, throat, or chest. Try listening to gentle music or nature sounds in the afternoon when energy dips, instead of reaching for caffeine.

If curiosity about devices arises—like auricular vagus nerve stimulators or HRV apps—test one for a single week. Don't shift other habits during your trial. Track whether it improves your calm scores or just adds noise. Remember, these tools may support but can't replace breath, touch, movement, or sound. Your body is the foundation (Fincham et al., 2023; Toussaint et al., 2021).

Graduation: Find Your Sustainable Core

Look back over your calm score notes from the past twelve weeks. Which techniques gave you the most ease? Pick one breath exercise, one touch or movement, and one sound or movement that felt reliable. Bundle these into a maintenance ritual—ten to fifteen minutes, placed at a steady point in your day. For busy stretches, create an emergency version: try two physiological sighs and a brief hand-on-heart pause. Set a recurring calendar reminder every month for a fifteen-minute review—scan your logs, adjust what isn't working, and celebrate even small wins. Your daily needs can change with seasons, jobs, parenting, or health. Flexibility keeps your practice useful (Toussaint et al., 2021).

For a busy parent, tracking in a notes app during naptime might work best. Someone managing work stress may keep their practice part of a morning routine before email. A caregiver could use an evening scan to transition out of work mode. If mornings don't work, try evenings or lunchtime instead. If five minutes feels out of reach, start with two—progress comes from showing up, not perfect streaks. Missing a day doesn't set you back; your nervous system learns from patterns, so returning the next day is what matters.

Keep your plan visible. Put a note on the fridge, snap a picture for your phone lock screen, or leave a sticky on your desk. This is both a reminder and a quiet celebration—the actions you repeat are shaping your resilience. Imagine yourself three months ahead, noticing stress sooner, choosing how to respond, and enjoying more moments of ease. Progress lives inside these small daily choices, made visible and possible by a plan tailored to you (Fincham et al., 2023; Toussaint et al., 2021).

CONCLUSION

You've reached the end of a journey that began with curiosity—or maybe, desperation. At its heart, this book set out to make the elusive vagus nerve real and approachable, putting the keys to nervous system health back in your hands. Together, we have moved from confusing medical jargon and myth-busting to actionable strategies grounded in science, all designed for daily life—not just theory. If you once felt frustration or overwhelm when anxiety struck, you now hold a living toolkit: practical ways to regulate your body and mind, gently and reliably. This transformation—from uncertainty to confidence—is yours, and it's worth celebrating.

Along the way, you learned to see anxiety not as a failing or a flaw but as a state that begins in the body: physical sensations that ripple upward, triggering thoughts and emotions. Understanding this sequence demystifies why old habits, like trying to "think your way calm," so often fell short. Now, you know how to meet rising stress at its source, armed with methods that directly engage the nervous system. The science is clear—small, compassionate interventions can interrupt spirals before they take root, offering relief that is fast, tangible, and sustainable.

These lessons were never just about information for its own sake. They form an integrated framework—a mosaic of biology, technology, mindfulness, and ancient wisdom.

You learned to blend breathing techniques that shift heart rhythms within seconds, cold and touch rituals that relay safety signals, sound and movement practices that invite connection, and gentler device-based supports if needed. No single tool stands alone; rather, these approaches layer, adapt, and strengthen one another. What once seemed a scattered assortment of wellness tips has become a personalized rhythm of care, flexible enough to respond to your needs on any given day.

If there was an 'aha' moment for many, perhaps it was realizing that nervous system change is possible at any stage of life. Neuroplasticity—the ability of your body and brain to rewire—means that nothing is fixed. Each slow exhale, gentle hum, or mindful pause lays down new pathways of resilience. You discovered that short, frequent practices are more potent than longer, exhausting ones, and that simplicity wins over struggle. Most empowering of all: you discovered agency. Anxiety is no longer an invisible enemy; it's a signal you can respond to, not just endure.

Your progress is real, whatever shape it takes. Whether you tracked calm scores in a journal, experimented with food and light tweaks, or bravely tried a cold splash at the end of a shower, these efforts add up to evidence of commitment. Completing this book is no small feat; it reflects dedication to learning, self-awareness, and personal growth. It means you valued your well-being enough to explore new science and test new skills—even when that meant facing discomfort or setbacks. Let yourself feel genuine pride; you've invested in something bigger than symptom relief—you've invested in lifelong resilience.

This ending isn't really an end—it's the beginning of a deeper relationship with your own body. Think of these pages as a springboard, not a finish line. As your life changes, so will your practice. There will be phases when routines feel easy, times when you need to dial back, and moments when bringing in a new micro-practice (or seeking outside support) makes sense. Consider engaging further: explore reputable apps for tracking HRV and mood, connect with trauma-aware therapists, or join online communities where others share stories of healing through holistic nervous system care. These resources expand your world and offer fresh perspectives whenever you need them.

Empowered with knowledge and firsthand experience, you now have the capacity to uplift those around you. Every success—however small—has ripple effects within families, workplaces, and neighborhoods. Your story might guide a friend struggling with panic, soothe worries for a child, or inspire a colleague to try a midday breathing break instead of powering through stress. Sharing what works for you—anchored in real science and lived results—helps combat misinformation while fostering cultures of self-kindness and mutual support. By modeling safety and inclusion, you contribute to communities where nervous system health isn't just a niche topic, but a shared value.

Thank you for letting this book join your journey. Writing these chapters, I imagined adults in coffee shops, parents reading between errands, professionals squeezing in a few mindful breaths before meetings—all searching for ways to bring calm into their lives. Anxiety's reality is never minimized here; its weight is hard, its reach unpredictable. But every page has been written in the hope that deepened understanding and gentle routines can restore not just composure, but joy. Please know that by reaching this point, you are part of a growing community—one that values courage, honesty, and care over quick fixes or empty promises.

As a closing invitation, choose one next step today. Perhaps revisit the 7-Day Calm Sprint introduced in Chapter 8, using your favorite two practices to anchor mornings and evenings. Or start your own nervous system profile (from Chapter 10), sketching out triggers and top soothers so your plan is ready for tomorrow. Don't aim for perfection; let consistency and self-compassion guide your pace. Progress unfolds in the small decisions you repeat, each act accumulating, day by day, into habits that protect and empower. May you move forward with confidence, knowing you have everything you need—and that your journey toward calm is uniquely, beautifully yours.

REFERENCE LIST

Aoyagi, K., Rivas, E., Shababi, R., Edwards, R., LaValley, M., Lechuga, J., Vitaly Napadow, & Tuhina Neogi. (2024, November 1). Safety and Preliminary Efficacy of Transcutaneous Auricular Vagus Nerve Stimulation on Chronic Knee Pain: A Pilot Trial. Osteoarthritis and Cartilage Open; Elsevier BV. https://doi.org/10.1016/j.ocarto.2024.100545

Afra, P., Adamolekun, B., Aydemir, S., & Watson, G. D. R. (2021, August 26). Evolution of the Vagus Nerve Stimulation (VNS) Therapy System Technology for Drug-Resistant Epilepsy. Frontiers in Medical Technology. https://doi.org/10.3389/fmedt.2021.696543

Balban, M. Y., Neri, E., Kogon, M. M., Weed, L., Nouriani, B., Jo, B., Holl, G., Zeitzer, J. M., Spiegel, D., & Huberman, A. D. (2023, January 10). Brief structured respiration practices enhance mood and reduce physiological arousal. Cell Reports Medicine. https://doi.org/10.1016/j.xcrm.2022.100895

Bentley, T. G. K., D'Andrea-Penna, G., Rakic, M., Arce, N., LaFaille, M., Berman, R., Cooley, K., & Sprimont, P. (2023, November 21). Breathing practices for stress and anxiety reduction: Conceptual framework of implementation guidelines based on a systematic review of the published literature. Brain Sciences. https://doi.org/10.3390/brainsci13121612

Bandealy, S. S., Sheth, N. C., Matuella, S. K., Chaikind, J. R., Oliva, I. A., Philip, S. R., Jones, P. M., & Hoge, E. A. (2021, June). Mind-Body Interventions for Anxiety Disorders: A Review of the Evidence Base for Mental Health Practitioners. FOCUS. https://doi.org/10.1176/appi.focus.20200042

Balaskas, A., Schueller, S. M., Doherty, K., Cox, A. L., & Doherty, G. (2024, June 1). Designing personalized mental health interventions for anxiety: CBT therapists' perspective. International Journal of Human-Computer Studies; Elsevier BV. https://doi.org/10.1016/j.ijhcs.2024.103319

Badran, B. W., & Austelle, C. W. (2022, January). The Future Is Noninvasive: A Brief Review of the Evolution and Clinical Utility of Vagus Nerve Stimulation. FOCUS. https://doi.org/10.1176/appi.focus.20210023

Beltzer, M. L., Meyerhoff, J., Popowski, S. A., Mohr, D. C., & Kornfield, R. (2023, October 6). Mental Health Self-Tracking Preferences of Young Adults With Depression and Anxiety Not Engaged in Treatment: Qualitative Analysis. JMIR Formative Research. https://doi.org/10.2196/48152

Badran, B. W., Yu, A. B., Adair, D., Mappin, G., DeVries, W. H., Jenkins, D. D., George, M. S., & Bikson, M. (2019, January 7). Laboratory Administration of Transcutaneous Auricular Vagus Nerve Stimulation (taVNS): Technique,

Targeting, and Considerations. Journal of Visualized Experiments. https://doi.org/10.3791/58984

Charles Ethan Paccione, & Henrik Børsting Jacobsen. (2019, June 11). Motivational Non-directive Resonance Breathing as a Treatment for Chronic Widespread Pain. Frontiers in Psychology; Frontiers Media. https://doi.org/10.3389/fpsyg.2019.01207

Can. (2025, October 13). Calm Blog. Calm Blog. https://www.calm.com/blog/ice-bath-benefits

Center for Substance Abuse Treatment (US). (2014). Exhibit 1.4-1, Grounding Techniques. Www.ncbi.nlm.nih.gov. https://www.ncbi.nlm.nih.gov/books/NBK207188/box/part1_ch4.box5/?report=objectonly

Center, M. H. (2025, September 3). Recognizing the Early Signs of a Mental Health Crisis | Mental Health Center. Mental Health Center. https://www.mentalhealthctr.com/recognizing-the-early-signs-of-a-mental-health-crisis/

Capilupi, M. J., Kerath, S. M., & Becker, L. B. (2020, February 1). Vagus Nerve Stimulation and the Cardiovascular System. Cold Spring Harbor Perspectives in Medicine. https://doi.org/10.1101/cshperspect.a034173

Center, B. A. C. (2024, February 14). Exploring T-Group: An Interpersonal Mindfulness Practice. Bay Area CBT Center. https://bayareacbtcenter.com/exploring-t-group-an-interpersonal-mindfulness-practice/

Curtiss, J. E., Levine, D. S., Ander, I., & Baker, A. W. (2021, June 17). Cognitive-behavioral treatments for anxiety and stress-related disorders. Focus. https://doi.org/10.1176/appi.focus.20200045

Dorsal Vagal Shutdown: How to Recognize When Your Nervous System Shuts Down. (2024, April 10). Neurodivergent Insights. https://neurodivergentinsights.com/dorsal-vagal-shutdown/?srsltid=AfmBOoqM7fgBH2rm5ArPlq7fVRoFyGROMPFmDPRMLB2oQQBCECoJsznI

Debnath, D. (2022, March 9). Visionify. Visionify AI Safety Solutions; Visionify Inc. https://visionify.ai/articles/unwind-after-work

Derricks, V., Pietri, E. S., Johnson, I. R., & Gonzalez, D. (2025, January 12). Examining the impact of identity-safety cues on inclusion for adults with higher body weights in healthcare settings. Patient Education and Counseling; Elsevier. https://doi.org/10.1016/j.pec.2025.108652

Evans, M., McDonald, A. C., Xiong, L., Crowley, D. C., & Guthrie, N. (2021, September 25). A Randomized, Triple-Blind, Placebo-Controlled, Crossover Study to Investigate the Efficacy of a Single Dose of AlphaWave®l-Theanine on Stress in a Healthy Adult Population. Neurology and Therapy. https://doi.org/10.1007/s40120-021-00284-x

Fooks, C., & Niebuhr, O. (2024, September 12). Effects of Vibroacoustic Stimulation on Psychological, Physiological, and Cognitive Stress. Sensors; Multidisciplinary Digital Publishing Institute. https://doi.org/10.3390/s24185924

Frykholm, E., Pettersson, B., Hedlund, M., Wiklund, M., Johansson, B., Carl-Johan Boraxbekk, Rosendahl, E., & Lindelöf, N. (2025, July 28). Supramaximal high-intensity interval training for older adults in a community setting: a pragmatic feasibility study. European Review of Aging and Physical Activity; BioMed Central. https://doi.org/10.1186/s11556-025-00379-6

Ferstl, M., Teckentrup, V., Lin, W. M., Kräutlein, F., Kühnel, A., Klaus, J., Walter, M., & Kroemer, N. B. (2021, February 15). Non-invasive vagus nerve stimulation boosts mood recovery after effort exertion. Psychological Medicine. https://doi.org/10.1017/s0033291720005073

Fincham, G. W., Kartar, A., Uthaug, M. V., Anderson, B., Hall, L., Nagai, Y., Critchley, H., & Colasanti, A. (2023, November 2). High ventilation breathwork practices: An overview of their effects, mechanisms, and considerations for clinical applications. Neuroscience and Biobehavioral Reviews. https://doi.org/10.1016/j.neubiorev.2023.105453

Galdino, A. (2025). Relaxation Techniques. a Practical Handbook for the Health Care Professional (2005). Scribd. https://www.scribd.com/document/386357439/Relaxation-Techniques-a-Practical-Handbook-for-the-Health-Care-Professional-2005

Gerritsen, R. J. S., & Band, G. P. H. (2018, October 9). Breath of Life: The Respiratory Vagal Stimulation Model of Contemplative Activity. Frontiers in Human Neuroscience. https://doi.org/10.3389/fnhum.2018.00397

Harjpal, P., Kovela, R. K., & Qureshi, M. I. (2023). Promoting Survival and Primitive Reflexes to Prevent Brain Imbalance in Premature Infants: A Scoping Review of New Insights by Physiotherapists on Developmental Disorders. Cureus. https://doi.org/10.7759/cureus.43757

How to Approach Sprints in Agile Project Management: 3 Recommendations. (2024). ICAgile. https://www.icagile.com/resources/how-to-approach-sprints-in-agile-project-management-3-recommendations

Hamdani, S. U., Huma, Z., Zafar, S. W., Suleman, N., Baneen, U., Waqas, A., & Rahman, A. (2022, June 28). Effectiveness of relaxation techniques "as an active ingredient of psychological interventions" to reduce distress, anxiety and depression in adolescents: a systematic review and meta-analysis. International Journal of Mental Health Systems. https://doi.org/10.1186/s13033-022-00541-y

Haynes, A. C., Lywood, A., Crowe, E. M., Fielding, J. L., Rossiter, J. M., & Kent, C. (2022, March 9). A calming hug: Design and validation of a tactile aid to ease anxiety. PLoS ONE. https://doi.org/10.1371/journal.pone.0259838

Henrique, Lécio Figueira Pinto, Daniela Fontes Bezerra, Luciano De Paola, Vassiliepe, F., Oliveira, A. J., Tayla Taynan Romão, Cristina, V., Silva, S., & D'Andrea-Meira, I. (2023, July 27). Predictive factors for successful vagus nerve stimulation in patients with refractory epilepsy: real-life insights from a multicenter study. Frontiers in Neuroscience; Frontiers Media. https://doi.org/10.3389/fnins.2023.1210221

Hamilton, V. (2025, October 22). How to Strengthen Your Vagal Tone and Calm Anxiety Naturally. Autoimmune Nutrition Clinic. https://theautoimmunitynutritionist.com/2025/10/22/how-to-strengthen-your-vagal-tone-and-calm-anxiety-naturally/

Jungmann, M., Vencatachellum, S., Van Ryckeghem, D., & Vögele, C. (2018, October 9). Effects of Cold Stimulation on Cardiac-Vagal Activation in Healthy Participants: Randomized Controlled Trial. JMIR Formative Research. https://doi.org/10.2196/10257

Keer, L. (2024, October 16). The Vagus Nerve: A Key Player in Your Health and Well-Being. Massachusetts General Hospital. https://www.massgeneral.org/news/article/vagus-nerve

Lindsay, E. K., Chin, B., Greco, C. M., Young, S., Brown, K. W., Wright, A. G. C., Smyth, J. M., Burkett, D., & Creswell, J. D. (2018, December). How mindfulness training promotes positive emotions: Dismantling acceptance skills training in two randomized controlled trials. Journal of Personality and Social Psychology. https://doi.org/10.1037/pspa0000134

Liu, H., & Boyatzis, R. E. (2021, June 24). Focusing on Resilience and Renewal From Stress: The Role of Emotional and Social Intelligence Competencies. Frontiers in Psychology. https://doi.org/10.3389/fpsyg.2021.685829

Lopez Blanco, C., & Tyler, W. J. (2025, July 11). The vagus nerve: a cornerstone for mental health and performance optimization in recreation and elite sports. Frontiers in

Psychology; Frontiers Media SA. https://doi.org/10.3389/fpsyg.2025.1639866

Lubbe, W., & ten Ham-Baloyi, W. (2017, April 27). When is the use of pacifiers justifiable in the baby-friendly hospital initiative context? A clinician's guide. BMC Pregnancy and Childbirth. https://doi.org/10.1186/s12884-017-1306-8

Leggett, H. (2023). "Cyclic sighing" can help breathe away anxiety. News Center. https://med.stanford.edu/news/insights/2023/02/cyclic-sighing-can-help-breathe-away-anxiety.html

Lai, J., Liu, J., Zhang, L., Cao, J., Hong, Y., Zhang, L., Fang, J., & Wang, X. (2025, February 6). Effect of transcutaneous vagus nerve stimulation with electrical stimulation on generalized anxiety disorder: Study protocol for an assessor-participant blinded, randomized sham-controlled trial. Heliyon; Elsevier. https://doi.org/10.1016/j.heliyon.2025.e42469

MEMT Dissertation and Thesis Catalog. (2025). Ku.edu. https://music.ku.edu/memt-dissertation-and-thesis-catalog

Myers, A. (2025, July 24). 12 science-backed vagus nerve exercises for anxiety relief. Thriveworks; Thriveworks Counseling. https://thriveworks.com/help-with/anxiety/vagus-nerve-exercises/

Miranda, G. (2023, March 7). Practice the Power of the Long Exhale. Mindful. https://www.mindful.org/practice-the-power-of-the-long-exhale/

Magnon, V., Dutheil, F., & Vallet, G. T. (2021). Benefits from one session of deep and slow breathing on vagal tone and anxiety in young and older adults. Scientific Reports. https://doi.org/10.1038/s41598-021-98736-9

Mauss, I. B., Zerwas, F. K., Wilhelm, F. H., & John, O. P. (2024, January 1). Coherence of emotional response systems: Theory, measurement, and benefits. Advances in Experimental Social Psychology; Elsevier BV. https://doi.org/10.1016/bs.aesp.2023.11.002

Ma, D., Li, C., Shi, W., Fan, Y., Liang, H., Li, L., Zhang, Z., & Yeh, C.-H. (2024, January 1). Benefits From Different Modes of Slow and Deep Breathing on Vagal Modulation. IEEE Journal of Translational Engineering in Health and Medicine; Institute of Electrical and Electronics Engineers. https://doi.org/10.1109/jtehm.2024.3419805

Murraysville, in. (2025, August 4). Pittsburgh Center for Integrative Therapy. Pittsburgh Center for Integrative Therapy. https://www.pittsburghcit.com/blog/somatic-practices

NHS. (2021, February 2). Breathing exercises for stress. Nhs.uk. https://www.nhs.uk/mental-health/self-help/guides-tools-and-activities/breathing-exercises-for-stress/

Nicholson, W. C., Sapp, M., Karas, E. M., Duva, I. M., & Grabbe, L. (2025, May 26). The Body Can Balance the Score: Using a Somatic Self-Care Intervention to Support Well-Being and Promote Healing. Healthcare; MDPI AG. https://doi.org/10.3390/healthcare13111258

Narjisse Damoun, Youssra Amekran, Taiek, N., & Abdelkader. (2024, August 1). Heart rate variability measurement and influencing factors: Towards the standardization of methodology. Global Cardiology Science and Practice; Magdi Yacoub Institute. https://doi.org/10.21542/gcsp.2024.35

Powers, M. B., SA, H., D, R., AL, P., HL, G., GV, C., JAJ, S., Warren, A. M., M, D., Naftalis, R., JG, W., M, F., MP, K., & RL, R. (2025, March 15). Vagus Nerve Stimulation Therapy for Treatment-Resistant PTSD. Brain Stimulation; Elsevier. https://doi.org/10.1016/j.brs.2025.03.007

Porges, S. W. (2022, May 10). Polyvagal Theory: a Science of Safety. Frontiers in Integrative Neuroscience. https://doi.org/10.3389/fnint.2022.871227

Resting heart rate before bed: the ultimate sleep metric • #1 Continuous Glucose Monitoring App Australia | Vively. (2025). Vively.co.uk. https://www.vively.co.uk/post/resting-heart-rate-before-bed-the-ultimate-sleep-metric

Ritchey, S. (2023, June 3). Understanding the Benefits of Reset Weeks for Fitness. Lemon8. https://www.lemon8-app.com/dr.shannon.dpt/7240542650967785990?region=us

Richer, R., Zenkner, J., Küderle, A., Rohleder, N., & Eskofier, B. M. (2022, November 10). Vagus activation by Cold Face Test reduces acute psychosocial stress responses. Scientific Reports. https://doi.org/10.1038/s41598-022-23222-9

Spa, B. (2023, November 15). Recognizing the Signs: Understanding When Crisis Intervention Is Needed.

Brain Spa. https://brainspallc.com/blog/recognizing-crisis-intervention-needed/

Sutton, J. (2023, October 17). Polyvagal theory explained (& 18 exercises & resources). PositivePsychology.com. https://positivepsychology.com/polyvagal-theory/

Shaffer, F., & Ginsberg, J. P. (2017, September 28). An Overview of Heart Rate Variability Metrics and Norms. Frontiers in Public Health. https://doi.org/10.3389/fpubh.2017.00258

Schuman-Olivier, Z., Trombka, M., Lovas, D. A., Brewer, J. A., Vago, D. R., Gawande, R., Dunne, J. P., Lazar, S. W., Loucks, E. B., & Fulwiler, C. (2020). Mindfulness and Behavior Change. Harvard Review of Psychiatry. https://doi.org/10.1097/HRP.0000000000000277

Suma. (2025, May 20). SMALL SHIFTS, BIG RELIEF: HOW TO CALM YOUR BODY, CONNECT WITH OTHERS AND CONQUER SOCIAL ANXIETY. National Social Anxiety Center. https://nationalsocialanxietycenter.com/2025/05/20/small-shifts-big-relief-calm-your-body-conquer-social-anxiety/

Smith, S. (2018). 5-4-3-2-1 Coping Technique for Anxiety. Www.urmc.rochester.edu. https://www.urmc.rochester.edu/behavioral-health-partners/bhp-blog/april-2018/5-4-3-2-1-coping-technique-for-anxiety

Team, E. (2024, July 5). COVID-19 Situation: Six Sigma Ongoing Training Announcements. SixSigma.us. https://www.6sigma.us/six-sigma-in-focus/agile-planning/

Tapita. (2025, September 23). 5 Power-Boosting Principles for Cycling Endurance (Plus the Science of Beetroot Powder). Stamox. https://stamox.com/en-no/blogs/health-performance/unlock-limitless-energy-5-power-boosting-principles-for-cycling-endurance?srsltid=AfmBOorojc2FpWAHN2WkpxZN3xCjltT5MbucSfG7ZXUoFdmm3GHfL32-

The 3 States of Anxiety in the Nervous System - Therapy in a Nutshell. (2022, November 11). https://therapyinanutshell.com/the-3-states-of-anxiety-in-the-nervous-system/

Toussaint, L., Nguyen, Q. A., Roettger, C., Dixon, K., Offenbächer, M., Kohls, N., Hirsch, J., & Sirois, F. (2021). Effectiveness of Progressive Muscle Relaxation, Deep Breathing, and Guided Imagery in Promoting Psychological and Physiological States of Relaxation (R. Taylor-Piliae, Ed.). Evidence-Based Complementary and Alternative Medicine. https://doi.org/10.1155/2021/5924040

Tiwari, R., Kumar, R., Malik, S., Raj, T., & Kumar, P. (2021, October 22). Analysis of Heart Rate Variability and Implication of Different Factors on Heart Rate Variability. Current Cardiology Reviews. https://doi.org/10.2174/1573403x16999201231203854

Updated Brain Death Guidance: What Care Teams Need to Know. (2025). Society of Critical Care Medicine (SCCM). https://www.sccm.org/communications/sccm-podcast/sccm-podcast-all-episodes/sccm-pod-533-ccm-updated-brain-death-guidance-what-critical-care-teams-need-to-know

Vagus Nerve | Psychology Today. (n.d.). Www. psychologytoday.com. https://www.psychologytoday.com/us/basics/vagus-nerve

eseospaceconsulting@gmail.com. (2025, July 4). Stress Response & Seasonal Fasting for Better Mental Wellness - Beata Lewis MD. Beata Lewis MD; Beata Lews MD. https://drlewis.com/stress-response-transformation/

vagus, schmagus! — waning crescent wellness. (2025, October 23). waning crescent wellness. Waning Crescent Wellness. https://www.waningcrescentwellness.com/blog/vagus-schmagus

www.ingramcontent.com/pod-product-compliance
Lightning Source LLC
Chambersburg PA
CBHW050528240926
51846CB00003B/731
* 9 7 8 1 9 8 9 8 0 5 2 0 6 *